SpringerBriefs on Cyber Security and Networks

Editor-in-Chief

Yang Xiang, Digital Research and Innovation Capability, Swinburne University of Technology, Hawthorn, Melbourne, VIC, Australia

Series editors

Liqun Chen, University of Surrey, Guildford, UK
Kim-Kwang Raymond Choo, University of Texas at San Antonio, San Antonio, TX, USA
Sherman S. M. Chow, Department of Information Engineering, The Chinese University of Hong Kong, Shatin, Hong Kong
Robert H. Deng, Singapore Management University, Singapore, Singapore
Dieter Gollmann, Hamburg University of Technology, Hamburg, Germany
Javier Lopez, University of Málaga, Málaga, Spain
Kui Ren, University at Buffalo, Buffalo, NY, USA
Jianying Zhou, Singapore University of Technology and Design, Singapore, Singapore

The series aims to develop and disseminate an understanding of innovations, paradigms, techniques, and technologies in the contexts of cyber security systems and networks related research and studies. It publishes thorough and cohesive overviews of state-of-the-art topics in cyber security, as well as sophisticated techniques, original research presentations and in-depth case studies in cyber systems and networks. The series also provides a single point of coverage of advanced and timely emerging topics as well as a forum for core concepts that may not have reached a level of maturity to warrant a comprehensive textbook. It addresses security, privacy, availability, and dependability issues for cyber systems and networks, and welcomes emerging technologies, such as artificial intelligence, cloud computing, cyber physical systems, and big data analytics related to cyber security research. The mainly focuses on the following research topics:

Fundamentals and Theories

- Cryptography for cyber security
- Theories of cyber security
- Provable security

Cyber Systems and Networks

- Cyber systems security
- Network security
- Security services
- Social networks security and privacy
- Cyber attacks and defense
- Data-driven cyber security
- Trusted computing and systems

Applications and Others

- Hardware and device security
- Cyber application security
- Human and social aspects of cyber security

More information about this series at http://www.springer.com/series/15797

Bo Liu · Wanlei Zhou · Tianqing Zhu
Yong Xiang · Kun Wang

Location Privacy in Mobile Applications

Bo Liu
La Trobe University
Bundoora, VIC, Australia

Wanlei Zhou
School of Software
University of Technology Sydney
Ultimo, NSW, Australia

Tianqing Zhu
School of Software
University of Technology Sydney
Ultimo, NSW, Australia

Yong Xiang
School of Information Technology
Deakin University
Burwood, VIC, Australia

Kun Wang
School of Internet of Things
Nanjing University of Posts
and Telecommunications
Nanjing, China

ISSN 2522-5561   ISSN 2522-557X   (electronic)
SpringerBriefs on Cyber Security Systems and Networks
ISBN 978-981-13-1704-0   ISBN 978-981-13-1705-7   (eBook)
https://doi.org/10.1007/978-981-13-1705-7

Library of Congress Control Number: 2018953315

This Springer imprint is published by the registered company Springer Nature Singapore Pte Ltd.
The registered company address is: 152 Beach Road, #21-01/04 Gateway East, Singapore 189721,
Singapore

Preface

The Global Positioning System (GPS) module has almost become standard in mobile phones in recent years, driving the growth of location-based services (LBSs) which provide a variety of information services (such as mobile social networks, navigation, places of interest finding, sports and healthy assistant, augmented reality games) based on the location data. As all the LBS providers require the access permission to users' location data, severe privacy concerns are raised at the same time. Therefore, effective location privacy preservation is foremost for these mobile applications.

Despite the big amount of papers in this area, there lacks a systematic study to present all related components of the problem. Moreover, the gap between theory and practice is big. To overcome these obstacles, this book will provide an integrated five-element framework for location privacy research, which includes analysis of location privacy definitions, attacks and adversaries, location privacy protection methods, location privacy metrics, and location-based mobile applications. In addition, we analyze the relationships between the different elements of location privacy. For example, a particular attack is targeted to the location data in a particular application. Then, it can be prevented by a certain type of protection method. Moreover, location privacy will be studied in detail in three different applications. We will also share some insights on the possible research directions.

We believe that this study will shed light on the research issues of location privacy and promote the advance and development of future location-based mobile applications. The content will be useful for researchers, students, and engineers in this area.

Melbourne, Australia   Bo Liu
June 2018

Contents

Acronyms

AR	Augmented reality
DP	Differential privacy
DSRC	Dedicated short-range communication
GPS	Global positioning system
LBA	Location-based application
LBS	Location-based service
LPPM	Location privacy preservation mechanism
MCS	Mobile crowd sensing
MSN	Mobile social network
OBU	On-board unit
PIR	Private information retrieval
POI	Place of interest
PSD	Personal sensing device
QoS	Quality of service
RoT	Region of Task
RSU	Roadside unit
SP	Service provider
SQL	Service quality loss
TTP	Trusted third party
V2R	Vehicle-to-roadside
V2V	Vehicle-to-vehicle
WAVE	Wireless Access for Vehicular Environments

Chapter 1
Introduction

This chapter introduces the basic concepts and the current research status of location privacy issues in mobile applications. It spans four aspects of study: the definition of location privacy, attacks and adversaries, people's view about the location privacy, and the current status of location-based applications. Through this comprehensive introduction, all the interrelated aspects of location privacy are integrated into a unified framework. And the links between existing academic research and its practical applications are identified. This chapter is designed to provide a foundation for the rest of the book.

The reminder of the chapter is organized as follows. Section 1.1 gives an brief introduction of the research background. Section 1.2 presents our definition of location privacy. In Sect. 1.3, we model the four aspects of adversaries and attacks. In Sect. 1.4, we discuss people's view about the location privacy issue and the current status of location privacy in terms of real-world applications in Sect. 1.5. Finally, we give the unified location privacy framework in Sect. 1.6 and conclude our work with a summary in Sect. 1.7.

1.1 Background

Global Positioning Systems (GPSs) are now a standard component in most cell phones, and their ubiquity is driving high growth in location-based information services (LBSs). According to statistics [1], in 2016, there were nearly 200 million LBS users in the USA. Inevitably, this upward trend will continue since LBSs fill many useful and interesting needs in a wide range of areas. Mobile social networks (Facebook, WeChat), navigation (Google Maps), finding places of interest (POI), sports and health assistants, and augmented reality (AR) games are just a few of the practical applications that have benefited from LBSs. In fact, for many businesses and government agencies, LBSs have become a critical part of deriving real insights from data tied to the specific locations where an activity takes place. However, accessing

© The Author(s), under exclusive licence to Springer Nature Singapore Pte Ltd. 2018
B. Liu et al., *Location Privacy in Mobile Applications*,
SpringerBriefs on Cyber Security Systems and Networks,
https://doi.org/10.1007/978-981-13-1705-7_1

personal location data, even with permission, raises severe privacy concerns for most users, and therefore, effective privacy preservation is foremost for LBS applications.

As a result, scholars have undertaken a great deal of research into ways of preserving the privacy of user locations. Various methods have been proposed, such as cryptography [2], anonymity [3], obfuscation [4, 5] and caching [6], but despite these efforts, there are still some obstacles to the progress of location privacy research:

- It is difficult to make comparisons between the different location privacy preservation mechanisms (LPPMs) because there is little consensus on the definition of location privacy or the best metrics to use to measure privacy levels.
- The gap between theory and practice is vast, with little analysis on how to implement LPPMs in real-world applications.

To overcome these obstacles, this book provides an updated and integrated framework for location privacy research. Based on the comprehensive review of the current location privacy protection researches, we will then focus on examples from three different mobile applications.

1.2 Definition of Location Privacy

LBSs pose the risk of location privacy disclosure because they rely on a variety of location information to provide their services. This section begins by introducing a generic system model of an LBS. Then, location privacy is defined within in this scope.

1.2.1 Location-Based Services

Figure 1.1 illustrates the general structure of an LBS. It contains the following components:

- A positioning system: GPS satellites are the most widely used positioning system. Cellular base stations and Wi-Fi routers can also be used as locating devices.
- Users: Most LBSs are distributed on mobile phones. However, LBSs are also frequently found in wearable devices and vehicles.
- Networks: Communication networks, including wireless local networks and cellular networks, are typically the first hop in the data transmission. Data are then usually transmitted over the Internet.
- LBS server: The LBS server responds to user queries and is usually operated and maintained by the LBS provider.
- Content/Data Provider: LBSs require massive amounts of data, such as POIs and maps. Some LBS providers own their own data and content, while others use a third party to provide this service.

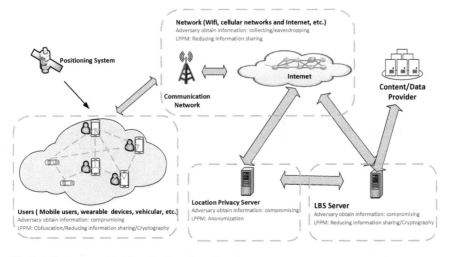

Fig. 1.1 System model of location based services

- Location privacy server: The location privacy server executes the privacy preservation algorithms, such as anonymization and encryption. This server can either be owned and operated by the LBS provider or by a third party.

The structure of the LBS dictates, in part, the possible types of attacks and adversaries a provider may confront. A more detailed discussion on this is provided in Sect. 1.3.

1.2.2 Representation of Location Information

From a privacy perspective, the location information in LBSs is not just a set of coordinates or the name of a place. It may also include the users' identity, spatial information (position), and temporal information (time). Hence, a users' location information can be defined as a tuple $< identity; position; time >$ [7, 8]. Each of these attributes can take different forms, as summarized in the following.

1.2.2.1 Identity

Identity is a users' name, email address, or any feature that makes a person distinguishable from another. In LBSs, identities can be either consistent or non-consistent [9] (Fig. 1.2).

Some LBSs require consistent user identities. For example, Pokemon Go requires its users to log in, while WeChats find my nearby friends function requires users to continuously provide their location information along with their WeChat ID [10].

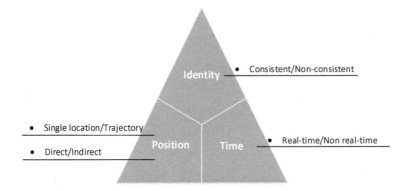

Fig. 1.2 Three attributes of the location information

Other LBSs do not require consistent user identities, or even the users' identity at all. For example, one can use Google Maps to find nearby restaurants anonymously or with a pseudonym.

An email address is the most common consistent identity required by LBSs. However, email addresses are an integral part of a users private information and can easily be used to conduct context linking attacks.

1.2.2.2   Spatial Information (Position)

Spatial information is the primary means of determining a location. Locations can either be described as a set of coordinates (e.g., longitude and latitude), or by some other form of information that can be linked to a location, such as a shop name. The different types of spatial information can be loosely divided into two categories:

Single locations and trajectories: Single locations are scattered and do not correlate to other locations. A trajectory is a group of locations with strong correlations, for example, a person trace.

Direct locations and indirect locations: Traditional LBSs, such as a check-in or nearby-POI services, use direct locations defined by GPS coordinates. Whereas, more recently, geo-social discovery services, which use indirect locations, have been rapidly growing in popularity. WeChat and Facebook contain good examples of these new types of services, where connections among users are explicitly established on-the-spot based on physical proximity. Rather than pinning down a users exact location on a map, proximity information is provided instead, such as "Tom is within 3 miles" [11].

1.2.2.3 Temporal Information (Time)

In addition to identity and location information, some LBSs also associated a time stamp with a location. Again, temporal information can be divided into two groups:

Non-real time: Some applications, such as Fitbit tracking, publish location or trajectory information afterward.

Real-time: Real-time privacy protection is more challenging than non-real-time protection because the scalability requirements in real-time privacy preservations become a much more important factor. Further, global optimization is very difficult with real-time information due to the highly dynamic and uncertain movements of users [9]. Examples of LBSs that use real-time location information include navigation and AR games.

1.2.3 The Definition of Location Privacy

Thus, location privacy can be defined as the protection of these three attributes of a persons location information. Blumberg et al. [12] use the following definition:

Location privacy *"is the ability of an individual to move in public space with the expectation that under normal circumstances their location will not be systematically and secretly recorded for later use".*

They also argue that there is no absolute location privacy, because:

...when you leave your home you sacrifice some privacy. Someone might see you enter the clinic on Market Street, or notice that you and your secretary left the Hilton Gardens Inn together.

According to this definition, location privacy has two main features: the individual's expectation of "normal circumstances", and the way the information is collected and used. However, a persons expectation of location privacy can change over time, especially with the rapid development of information technology and the dramatic increase in the amount of location information that is used in everyday life. Additionally, the ways we collect and use location information has also changed. Today, personal information is more often collected quietly by inconspicuous devices, such as mobile phones, RFID tags, and cameras [13]. Moreover, newly emerging technologies, such as machine/deep learning and face recognition, have also changed how location data can be used to derive more sensitive personal information.

Therefore, to evaluate the privacy of a location, its key factors must be defined from the users' point of view:

- How: how is the information revealed? Is it revealed secretly or publicly? Is it encrypted or not? And how will the information be used?
- What: what kind of information is revealed? Is it a set of coordinates, at a particular time, and with my identity attached? Are these attributes precise or coarse?

These two key factors also form the basis of our investigation into the features of attacks and adversaries in the next section of the paper.

1.2.4 Location Privacy Versus Data Privacy

Location privacy is a subcategory of data privacy. Among the different types of personal data categories, the risks of unsanctioned disclosures of financial and medical records are well-known. However, risks associated with location are no less grave for the following reasons:

- Identity inference: Location data holds a unique capacity to link disparate datasets in a way that can reveal personally identifiable information through inference. And these links only rely on an understanding of the relationships between data and human activity.
- Profiling completeness: User locations typically contain POIs, such as hospitals and restaurants. Thus, one may be able to gain a deeper understanding of user behavior in the real world and use that data to predict future activity. The ability of location information to "connect the dots" almost automatically results in a much more complete profile of an individual or organization than the base data contains.

Location data also hold some distinguishing characteristics. Location data are typically:

- Massive: Using an LBS generates enormous amounts of location data, no matter the form.
- Highly correlated: A real-world location dataset often exhibits strong coupling relations; locations are often correlated, and these correlations may disclose more information than expected.
- Dynamic: The data can change quickly over time.
- Unequal in importance: From a users' point of view, their privacy requirements differ from location to location. For example, most people care very little about exposing the location of a shopping center visit, but care very much about keeping their home and workplace secret.

These features require special attention when conducting location privacy studies.

1.3 Location Attacks and Adversaries

An adversary aims to collect location information and use it for their benefit. Based on the two key factors of location privacy, an adversary and their attack can be characterized by "how" they obtained the information, "how" the attack is launched, "what" information or knowledge they obtained, and "what/who" their target is. Figure 1.3 illustrates this four-part model of an adversary and an attack. Each aspect of the model will be analyzed in detail in this section.

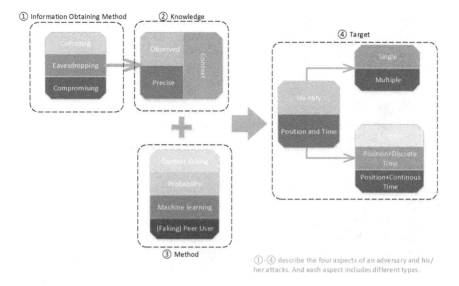

Fig. 1.3 An overview of the location attacks and adversaries

1.3.1 Location Information Obtaining Methods

As shown in Fig. 1.1, the three main parties in an LBS system are the users, the servers, and the networks. Each party can be attacked, and each attack can be measured and categorized by its victim and level of danger.

1. Collecting shared or published location information, historical statistics, or distributions. Some attacks can be as simple as collecting published data using tools like a Web Crawler.
2. Eavesdropping on a network (communication channel) can expose the data traffic between the server and client or between clients (e.g., peer-to-peer networks), especially with the wireless networks.
3. Compromising the server or the client through a hack that extracts any information an adversary wants.

1.3.2 Types of Adversarial Knowledge

Once an adversary has acquired some location information, through whatever means, they may hold the necessary knowledge to carry out a location attack. However, the power of this knowledge depends on whether it has been processed through a privacy preservation scheme.

- Observed location information has been preprocessed by the user, a third-party privacy server, or the service provider before being divulged. It may still be vulnerable to exploitation, but is less vulnerable than precise information.
- Precise location information has not been processed and is vulnerable to compromise and hacks.

In addition, an adversary may have other knowledge that can be used to help breach location privacy. This additional knowledge is referred to as

- Context knowledge: any information that could be used by an adversary to help reveal the location information of a user.

Examples of contextual knowledge include (1) the number of users in an area at a given time; (2) the relationships between different users; (3) the relationships between a users' identity and their location; (4) the location restrictions of an area, such as road networks and POIs; (5) the statistical distributions or probabilities associated with a location (e.g., people tend to stay home at night); and (6) social event information (e.g., well-publicized events held by, say, a celebrity or museum).

1.3.3   Attack Targets

The first type of attack is the self-explanatory *identity attack*. *Localization attack* combine spatial and temporal information as targets because this information is often highly related.

1.3.3.1   Identity Attack

Identity attacks, also known as deanonymizing attacks, seek information for the purposes of determining a targets identity. Examples of these types of attacks include

- Personal identification attack (single identity attack): identifying a user based on their home address [14], or determining a persons gender and education, for example, through an anonymous trace [11].
- Meeting Disclosure Attacks/Aggregated Presence Attack (multiple identity attacks): inferring the relationship between two people or an aggregated property, for example, whether two people met on a certain day or the approximate number of people visiting a Pokemon Go stop.

1.3.3.2   Localization Attack

Localization attacks focus on determining *position* and *time* information. Some examples follow.

- Sensitive place attacks (position attack): identifying important locations, such as home and work [15, 16].
- Presence and absence disclosure attack (position and discrete time attack): determining whether or not a user is present at a place at a specific time. For instance, empty homes are good targets for burglary; physically attacking a person requires you know where they are [17, 18].
- Tracking attack (position and continuous time attack): assembling a partial or entire sequence of the events to develop a user trace. This kind of adversary is generally known as stalking [19–21].

1.3.4 Types of Attack Methods

Lastly, adversaries can use different methods of attack.

- Context linking attacks: Most location attacks involve some contextual knowledge. Contextual knowledge is easy to combine with the observed location information to obtain a precise location for a target, for the purposes of conducting a localization attack. For instance, in a personal context linking attack [3], which can be used to reduce an obfuscated area to a specific location and then locate users by removing all the irrelevant areas. Contextual knowledge can also be combined with precise location information to conduct an identity attack. For example, if an adversary knows a persons home address and finds that address in a hospitals check-in list, the adversary can infer that their target is, or was, in that hospital at a specific time.
- Probability-based attacks: Probability distribution attacks [22] are based on gathered statistics about environmental contexts. A Markov chain model is widely used in these type of attacks. Using this method, an adversary can either perform a localization attack (location prediction [23]) or an identity attack (de-anonymization [24]). Strictly speaking, statistical information is actually a kind of contextual information; however, since exploiting probability theory is an important category of attacks, we have discussed it separately.
- Machine/deep learning-based attacks: Li et al. [11] proposed an approach to inferring user demographics in a mobile social network (MSN) based on machine learning. The type of demographic information included gender and education level, and their experiments demonstrated a 70% successful rate on a large real-world dataset. Murakami et al. [25] proposed a learning method that uses tensor factorization to accurately estimate personalized transition matrices from a small amount of training data. The matrices are then used to launch a localization attack that can derive the actual location of a user at a given time from an obfuscated trajectory.

  In a recent work [26], Weyand et al. showed that it is possible to determine the location of a photograph by its pixels alone using a convolutional neural network.
- Collusion of malicious users attacks: Peers subscribing to the same LBS can either collude to launch attacks, or one adversary can create fake peers to obtain the infor-

mation they seek. For example, Li et al. [27] created three fake anchor locations and used their corresponding distances to the target in an iterative trilateration based on a localization algorithm to obtain an inferred location.

1.3.5 Emerging Trends

Big data and deep learning techniques are changing the landscape of location privacy. In particular, two attack trends have become more challenging than ever before cross-database and platform attacks and deep learning attacks. Cross-database and platform attacks exploit the links between the location information in two different databases to infer sensitive information about their target. The unprecedented accuracy of deep learning methods is also posing significant challenges. For example, current deep learning-based methods are able to predict geolocations [26] from personal photographs posted on social networks. These trends are likely to become the increasing focus of future research.

1.4   People's View About Location Privacy

People's views on location privacy changes over time. Studies prior to 2010 [28–30] show that the general public were not very concerned about their location privacy. However, with the boom of LBSs in recent years, new research has been conducted that tells a different story.

Below, we summarize these opinions in two different respects.

1.4.1 Do People Really Know How Much of Their Location Information Has Been Collected or Revealed?

Some researchers argue that people do not much care about their location privacy because they are often unaware of the amount and frequency of the data collected by their applications. Aalmuhammed et al. [31] show that a user's location can be shared more than 5000 times in a two-week period. And participants in the study knew how frequently their data were being collected, 95% of them reassessed their permissions, and 58% further restricted some of their permissions.

1.4.2 How Do People Care About Their Location Privacy?

Fawaz et al. [32] surveyed 180 smartphone users. 78% of the participants believe that apps accessing their location can pose privacy threats. Also, 85% of them reported that they care about who accesses their location information. 77% of the users included the term "privacy" as a factor affecting their choice in installing a privacy protection mechanism.

Thus, we cannot arbitrarily assert that people care or do not care about their location privacy nowadays. In most cases, people are weighing the price of information sharing with the corresponding benefits. As people become more aware of the risk of disclosing their location information, it is reasonable to believe that the majority of the public will pay more attention to location privacy issues.

1.5 Location-Based Services in Practical Applications

LBSs experienced a boom along with the emergence of the smartphone and are currently widely used in a variety of contexts, such as health, entertainment, work, and personal life. According to the different application scenarios, current LBSs can be grouped into the following categories [33]:

- Geo-social services [34]: These services have introduced location information into social networking platforms to enrich interactivity and the relationships between people. The very first service of this kind was the check-in service. Foursquare [35] was one of the earliest LBS applications to provide a check-in function. Glympse is a similar application, and there are many others [36]. This simple check-in concept was soon extended to encompass a broader vision of geo-social services, including location sharing among friends (Foursquare), posting geo-tagged tweets (Twitter [37]) or moments (Wechat), and to finding nearby friends (WeChat, Facebook).
- Information services: Current navigation systems provide real-time traffic condition reports and route selection based on a users' location. Passengers can obtain public transport timetables at bus stops and train stations. Additionally, some services provide nearby-POI information to their users. Yelp [38] was one of the first online local POI search services. Its mobile version provides an easy way for users to find nearby POIs by allowing Yelp to access to their current location. Similarly, many other traditional Web-based services, such as Tripadvisor [39], have LBS versions for mobile platforms. In addition, unmanned autonomous systems, or autonomous systems for short, are becoming mainstream in practice, with the widespread introduction of autonomous vehicles, drones, and so on. These systems also include LBSs.
- Healthcare assistant systems: Fitbit [40] is an example of this type of LBS, which is an activity tracker and a wireless-enabled wearable technology device that measures data, such as the number of steps walked, heart rate, quality of sleep, steps climbed, and other personal metrics involved in fitness.

- Augmented reality (AR) games: While the craze has cooled somewhat, Pokemon Go [41] has launched a new era of AR games by combining the addictive creature collection and monster battling play in Nintendos Pokemon with Niantics augmented reality technology. Players explore their neighborhood on foot, using their smartphone as a map and viewfinder to discover and collect Pokemon. Pokemon, and their accoutrements, can also be collected from Pokestops shops and gyms tied to real-world locations that you need to physically travel to which encourages players to explore their neighborhood and get their feet in gear.

The above summary of categories is based on the functions and aims of the services, but different LBSs use different types of location information as well. Table 1.1 lists the types of location information used in the different LBSs.

The current trend is to integrate multiple functions into one application. For example, the original Foursquare has become a location-aware smart-search tool that focuses on discovering nearby locations, events, restaurants, and shops, while Swarm caters to those addicted to checking in and location sharing with friends. Google Maps has paired its navigation system with location awareness functions that allow you to easily find everything you need, like nearby POIs, traffic, and the estimated travel time to any destination.

To distinguish the application from the provided service, we have used the term location-based application (LBA) to refer to any device, software, or mobile app that provides an LBS. Given that one LBA can house multiple LBSs, the types of LBSs provided in popular LBAs have been provided in Table 1.2) as general context.

Table 1.1 Summary of location information types in the current LBS applications

LBS Name		Identity information	Spatial information	Temporal information
Geo-social services	Check-in geo-tagged posters finding nearby friends	C*	$S^\dagger, D^\dagger$	$NR^\$$
		C	S, D	$R^\$$
		C	S, I	R
Geo-information services	Navigation finding POI	NC*	$S, T^\dagger, D$	R
		NC	S, T, D, I	R, NR
Sports and health assistant	Sports tracking	C	T, D	R
Augmented reality (AR) games	Pokemon Go	C	T, I	R

∗ Consistent: C; Non-consistent: NC.
† Single: S; Trajectory: T; Direct: D; Indirect: I.
$ Real-time: R; Non-real-time: NR.

Table 1.2 Summary of LBSs provided by different LBAs

LBA name	Check-in	Geo-tagged posters	Finding nearby friends	Navigation	Finding POI	Sports tracking	AR Game
Foursquare	✓		✓		✓		
Facebook	✓		✓		✓		
Twitter		✓					
Google maps				✓	✓		
Wechat		✓	✓				
Pokemon Go							✓
Fitbit						✓	
Yelp	✓				✓		

Fig. 1.4 Connections of different aspects of the location privacy

1.6   The Unified Location Privacy Research Framework

To overcome these obstacles, this study provides an updated and integrated framework for location privacy research [42]. It includes location privacy definitions, and reviews of attacks and adversaries, LPPMs, location privacy metrics, and the applications that rely on location privacy. In addition, we analyze the relationships between the different aspects of location privacy (Fig. 1.4), for example, the types of attacks that target particular attributes of location privacy but can be prevented by a certain type of LPPM or evaluated with a certain metric.

1.7   Outline and Book Overview

This chapter is an overview of the location privacy including the definition, attacks, peoples view, and the related applications. Chapter 2 summarizes and compares the current location privacy-preserving mechanisms, which provides a foundation to the following chapters. Chapters 3–5 investigate the location privacy protection in three different applications in detail. Chapter 6 discusses the future research directions and concludes the whole book.

References

1. U.S. location-based service users, https://www.statista.com/statistics/436071/location-based-service-users-usa/. Accessed 19 Dec 2016
2. G. Ghinita, P. Kalnis, A. Khoshgozaran, C. Shahabi, K.-L. Tan, Private queries in location based services: anonymizers are not necessary, in *Proceedings of the ACM SIGMOD* (2008), pp. 121–132
3. M. Gruteser, D. Grunwald, Anonymous usage of location-based services through spatial and temporal cloaking, in *Proceedings of the ACM MobiSys* (2003), pp. 31–42
4. H. Kido, Y. Yanagisawa, T. Satoh, An anonymous communication technique using dummies for location-based services, in *Proceedings of the IEEE ICPS* (2005), pp. 88–97
5. C.A. Ardagna, M. Cremonini, S.D.C. di Vimercati, P. Samarati, An obfuscation-based approach for protecting location privacy. IEEE Trans. Dependable and Secur. Comput. **8**(1), 13–27 (2011)
6. B. Niu, Q. Li, X. Zhu, G. Cao, H. Li, Enhancing privacy through caching in location-based services, in *Proceedings of the IEEE INFOCOM* (2015)
7. K. Barker, M. Askari, M. Banerjee, K. Ghazinour, B. Mackas, M. Majedi, S. Pun, A. Williams, A data privacy taxonomy, in *British National Conference on Databases* (Springer, Berlin, 2009), pp. 42–54
8. M. Wernke, P. Skvortsov, F. Dürr, K. Rothermel, A classification of location privacy attacks and approaches. Pers. Ubiquitous Comput. **18**(1), 163–175 (2014)
9. C.-Y. Chow, M.F. Mokbel, Privacy of spatial trajectories, in *Computing with Spatial Trajectories* (Springer, Berlin, 2011), pp. 109–141
10. Wechat (2019), https://www.wechat.com. Accessed 19 Dec 2016
11. H. Li, H. Zhu, S. Du, X. Liang, X. Shen, Privacy leakage of location sharing in mobile social networks: attacks and defense. IEEE Trans. Dependable Secur. Comput. **1**, 1–1 (2016)
12. A.J. Blumberg, P. Eckersley, On locational privacy, and how to avoid losing it forever. Electron. Frontier Found. **10**(11) (2009)
13. Why location privacy is important (2030), http://www.itworld.com/article/2752981/mobile/why-location-privacy-is-important.html. Accessed 30 Nov 2016
14. J. Krumm, Inference attacks on location tracks, in *Proceedings of the IEEE Percom* (2007), pp. 127–143
15. Y. Gu, Y. Yao, W. Liu, J. Song, We know where you are: Home location identification in location-based social networks, in *Proceedings of the ICCCN* (IEEE, 2016), pp. 1–9
16. J. Mahmud, J. Nichols, C. Drews, Home location identification of twitter users. ACM Trans. Intell. Syst. Technol. **5**(3), 47 (2014)
17. How burglars use facebook to target vacationing homeowners (2013), http://www.ibtimes.com/how-burglars-use-facebook-target-vacationing-homeowners-1341325. Accessed 30 Nov 2016
18. J. Bellatti, A. Brunner, J. Lewis, P. Annadata, W. Eltarjaman, R. Dewri, R. Thurimella, Driving habits data: location privacy implications and solutions. IEEE Secur. Priv. **15**(1), 12–20 (2017)

19. Tracing a stalker (2013), http://www.nbcnews.com/id/19253352/#.WDexmYVOLD4. Accessed 30 Nov 2016
20. Authorities: GPS system used to stalk woman (2013), http://usatoday30.usatoday.com/tech/news/2002-12-30-gps-stalker_x.htm. Accessed 30 Nov 2016
21. Steven brown used GPS devices and private detectives to stalk his estranged partner (2030), http://www.dailyecho.co.uk/news/14920127.Stalker_used_GPS_devices_and_private_detectives_to_stalk_his_estranged_partner/. Accessed 30 Nov 2016
22. R. Shokri, G. Theodorakopoulos, J.-Y. Le Boudec, J.-P. Hubaux, Quantifying location privacy, in *Proceedings of the IEEE Symposium on Security and Privacy* (2011), pp. 247–262
23. K. Minami, N. Borisov, Protecting location privacy against inference attacks, in *Proceedings of the ACM Workshop on Privacy in the Electronic Society* (2010), pp. 123–126
24. S. Gambs, M.-O. Killijian, M.N. del Prado Cortez, De-anonymization attack on geolocated data. J. Comput. Syst. Sci. **80**(8), 1597–1614 (2014)
25. T. Murakami, H. Watanabe, Localization attacks using matrix and tensor factorization. IEEE Trans. Inf. Forensics Secur. **11**(8), 1647–1660 (2016)
26. T. Weyand, I. Kostrikov, J. Philbin, Planet-photo geolocation with convolutional neural networks, in *European Conference on Computer Vision* (Springer, Berlin, 2016), pp. 37–55
27. M. Li, H. Zhu, Z. Gao, S. Chen, L. Yu, S. Hu, K. Ren, All your location are belong to us: breaking mobile social networks for automated user location tracking, in *Proceedings of the ACM International Symposium on Mobile Ad Hoc Networking and Computing*, 2014, pp. 43–52
28. M. Colbert, A diary study of rendezvousing: implications for position-aware computing and communications for the general public, in *Proceedings of the ACM SIGGROUP Conference on Supporting Group Work* (2001), pp. 15–23
29. E. Kaasinen, User needs for location-aware mobile services. Pers. Ubiquitous Comput. **7**(1), 70–79 (2003)
30. G. Danezis, S. Lewis, R.J. Anderson, How much is location privacy worth? in *WEIS* (Citeseer), vol. 5 (2005)
31. H. Almuhimedi, F. Schaub, N. Sadeh, I. Adjerid, A. Acquisti, J. Gluck, L.F. Cranor, Y. Agarwal, Your location has been shared 5,398 times!: a field study on mobile app privacy nudging, in *Proceedings of the ACM Conference on Human Factors in Computing Systems* (2015), pp. 787–796
32. K. Fawaz, K.G. Shin, Location privacy protection for smartphone users, in *Proceedings of the ACM SIGSAC Conference on Computer and Communications Security* (2014), pp. 239–250
33. Mobile location apps review (2030), http://www.webmapsolutions.com/mobile-location-apps/. Accessed 30 Nov 2016
34. C.R. Vicente, D. Freni, C. Bettini, C.S. Jensen, Location-related privacy in geo-social networks. IEEE Internet Comput. **15**(3), 20–27 (2011)
35. Foursqure (2021), https://foursquare.com/. Accessed 21 Dec 2016
36. Glympse (2021), https://www.glympse.com/. Accessed 21 Dec 2016
37. twitter (2021), https://twitter.com/. Accessed 21 Dec 2016
38. Yelp (2019), https://www.tripadvisor.com.au/. Accessed 19 Dec 2016
39. Tripadvisor (2002), https://www.yelp.com.au/. Accessed 02 Jan 2017
40. Fitbit (2019), https://www.fitbit.com. Accessed 19 Dec 2016
41. Pokemon go (2019), http://www.pokemongo.com/. Accessed 19 Dec 2016
42. B. Liu, W. Zhou, T. Zhu, L. Gao, Y. Xiang, Location privacy and its applications: a systematic study, in *IEEE Access*, vol. 6 (2018), pp. 17606–17624

Chapter 2
Location Privacy-Preserving Mechanisms

This chapter reviews the existing location privacy-preserving mechanisms (LPPMs). There have been some survey papers discussing this topic. For example, Shokri et al. [1] discuss LPPMs in two groups: obfuscation mechanisms and anonymization mechanisms. Our review of the literature reveals two further mechanisms, cryptographic mechanisms and shared information reduction mechanisms, creating four categories for existing LPPMs [2].

Sections 2.1–2.4 introduces LPPMs in these four categories, respectively. We also compare the different LPPMs in Sect. 2.5. Finally, Sect. 2.6 lists the frequently used metrics in LPPM performance evaluations.

2.1 Cryptographic Mechanism

LPPMs based on cryptography use encryption to protect user positions. Mascetti et al. [3] proposed an approach to notify users when their friends, called buddies, are in proximity but without revealing the current user's position to the LBS server. To this end, the authors assume that each user shares a secret with each of his buddies through a symmetric encryption technique. Another approach proposed by Ghinita et al. [4] makes use of a private information retrieval (PIR) technique to provide location privacy. Through PIR, an LBS server can answer queries without learning or revealing any information about the query. PIR relies on an assumption of quadratic residuosity, which states that it is computationally hard to find quadratic residues in the modulo arithmetic of a large composite number for the product of two large primes. To deal with the problem of non-trusted LBS server infrastructures, Marias et al. [5] proposed an approach based on distributing the position information and secret sharing. The basic idea is to divide the position information into shares, which are then distributed among a set of (non-trusted) LBS servers. Hence, to reassemble the position information, the client needs to retrieve the shares from multiple servers. The advantage of this approach is that compromising one LBS server will not reveal

© The Author(s), under exclusive licence to Springer Nature Singapore Pte Ltd. 2018   17
B. Liu et al., *Location Privacy in Mobile Applications*,
SpringerBriefs on Cyber Security Systems and Networks,
https://doi.org/10.1007/978-981-13-1705-7_2

the position information since it does not have all the necessary shares. However, the downside is that none of the LBS servers can perform computations that require all the position information, such as range queries.

Chen et al. [6] constructed a secure query protocol, where different data providers can use different secret keys to encrypt their data to prevent the location server from deducing the content of the query data.

The main concerns with cryptographic mechanism are their computational complexity and/or the requirement of cooperative servers. It is worth noting that this area of research has not seen any great breakthroughs for some time.

2.2   Anonymization Mechanisms

These types of methods aim to break the links between identity and location information. They mainly fall into two categories: k-anonymity and mix-zone.

2.2.1   k-Anonymity

k-anonymity [7–11] achieves privacy preservation through generalization and suppression algorithms to ensure that one record cannot be distinguished from $(k - 1)$ to the other records. A subject is considered k-anonymous if its location is indistinguishable from those of $k - 1$ other users.

The basic concept of k-anonymity [7] requires that the location privacy server is operated by a trusted third party (TTP). This trusted LBS server is aware of all precise user positions and acts as the anonymizer. Whenever a user needs to transmit their location along with a query, the TTP calculates a set of k users and reports an obfuscation area containing k positions including that of the querying user.

k-anonymity has been extended in two directions. The first direction attempts to avoid a single trusted anonymizer, either by employing multiple distributed servers [12, 13] or using peer-to-peer communication instead of a server [14]. The second direction constrains which users are included in k based on a set of conditions relating to the potential contextual knowledge an adversary may have. For example, *p-sensitivity*, [15], aims to guarantee the key attributes have at least p different values within the k user set (i.e., an identity information constraint). *l-diversity*, [16, 17], ensures that the location of the user is unidentifiable from a set of l different physical locations (i.e., a location information constraint). And *historical k-anonymity*, [18], provides guarantees for moving objects (i.e., a time information constraint).

k-anonymization approaches are targeted at the applications that do not demand a true or pseudo identity, such as finding nearby gas stations or restaurants, or notifying a user of the sale price of items as they pass through a shopping mall. The basic concept is to break the link between the identity and the location by hiding this information among similar anonymous users. However, k-anonymization techniques are ineffective when the LBS relies on some form of identity information to deliver its services because this information in association with spatially cloaked regions is vulnerable to inference attacks [19, 20].

2.2.2 Mix-Zone

Unlike k-anonymity, mix-zones can be used without user identity information. The first mix-zone approach was proposed by Beresford [21] Here, the privacy of the user is maintained by constantly changing the user's name or pseudonym within a mix-zone. Since then, this method has been investigated in the context of several different applications. Ying et al. [22] proposed a dynamic mix-zone for location privacy in vehicular networks, which dynamically forms the mix-zone at the time the vehicle requests it. The MobiMix approach proposed by Palanisamy et al. [20] is a mix-zone framework based on road networks that considers the anonymization effectiveness and resilience of timing and transition attacks. Lu et al. [23] incorporate pseudonym changes at social spots to achieve location privacy, while Gao et al. [24] use a mix-zone framework that hides the exact location information within a designed trajectory mix-zone for mobile crowd sensing (MCS) applications. Xu et al. [25] treated the problem of optimal multiple mix-zones as a transportation problem and built a mixed-integer programming model with the objective of minimizing the amount of time the users' privacy level is lower than their privacy requirement.

Both the k-anonymity and mix-zone schemes require users to cooperate to reach a target level of privacy, thus inspiring research on incentives for cooperation. For example, Freudiger et al. [26] model the behavior of mobile nodes as pseudonyms change in a noncooperative game where each player aims to maximize their location privacy for minimum cost. Gong et al. [27] modeled user decision making about whether to change pseudonyms as a socially aware pseudonym change game. Auction-based mechanisms were designed in [28] to impel users to participate in pseudonym change. Gong et al. [29] assumed a general anonymity model that allows a user to have their specific anonymity set to a personalized level of location privacy using a social group utility approach.

Anonymization has been well studied and applied to many different scenarios. However, this approach has also attracted some criticisms [30]. The main concern is that it is unreasonable to maintain the same level of anonymity in different contexts. For example, a group of users cooperating to achieve k-anonymity may either be near each other in a small place (e.g., a train station) or in the opposite situation and scattered across a large area. k-anonymity is satisfied in both cases, but it is clear that the users in the second case have better location privacy because an adversary would have more uncertainty about their exact locations. This example also implies that k is sometimes irrelevant to actual location privacy.

2.3   Obfuscation Mechanisms

Obfuscation mechanisms encompass a range of methods that reduce the precision of location information. Some add dummy locations, others perturb (add noise), and still others reduce the granularity of the information [1, 31, 32].

2.3.1   Dummy Locations

The goal of position dummies is to mask a user's true position by sending multiple false positions (dummies) to the LBS server together with the true position [33]. Since the dummy locations are randomly selected from the user's mobile device, this method does not require any trusted servers and is known to achieve good levels of privacy without loss of accuracy.

The classic dummy method only addressed single locations but has since been extended to trajectories. You et al.'s [34] method produces a user's dummy trajectories through random or rotating patterns. Specifically, the random pattern generates dummy trajectories beginning with the starting point and moving toward the destination. The rotating patterns cycle through a set of dummy user trajectories. In [35], Lei et al. use a rotation scheme to rotate a user trajectory that satisfies the distance deviation to make the actual user trajectory indistinguishable from the dummies.

Given that an adversary may have additional contextual knowledge, such as the map of a certain area, some research efforts have focused on improving the dummy location method to create dummies that not only are realistic but also cannot be distinguished from the user's true position. Krumm [36] faked a users' driving movements using a database of actual GPS tracks from 253 drivers. To make the model more realistic, they also compute the probability of a given position being a plausible start or end point. Chow et al. [37] generated fake location traces by leveraging Google Maps. They add simulated stops and noise in the routes planned by Google Maps and output a fraction of the points according to the desired time range. Do et al. [38] proposed a dummy generation method using conditional probabilities to generate realistic false locations that are resistant to adversaries who have information about the user as well as external spatiotemporal knowledge. Hara et al. [39] proposed a method to generate natural dummies that consider the physical constraints of the real environment.

2.3.2   Location Obfuscation

Spatial obfuscation approaches attempt to preserve privacy by deliberately reducing the precision of the position information sent from the user to the LBS server and, in turn, to the client. A classic spatial obfuscation approach is the one presented by

Ardagna et al. [40, 41], where a user sends a circular area instead of the precise user position to the LBS server. Gutscher et al. [42] proposed an approach based on coordinate transformation, where the mobile device performs some simple geometric operations on their positions (e.g., shifting, rotating) before sending them to the LBS server.

These location obfuscation methods, designed to protect spatial information, led researchers to investigate ways of protecting temporal information. Hwang et al. [43] introduced a novel time-obfuscating technique that issues multiple user queries at different times to confuse the LBS. By sending a query randomly from a set of random trajectories based on the user's location, the LBS cannot know the user's real trajectory. Terrovitis et al. [44] considered spatiotemporal obfuscation to protect the published trajectories of users. A similar idea was presented by Ghinita et al. [45] in their spatiotemporal cloaking approach.

There are some papers that consider more complex adversarial knowledge. Duckham and Kulik used obfuscation graphs to apply the concept of location obfuscation to road networks [46]. Ghinita et al. [45] considered background map knowledge represented by a set of privacy-sensitive features. Xiao et al. [47] developed a framework to preserve location privacy that accounts for the temporal correlations in location data.

2.3.3 Differential Privacy-Based Methods

The application of differential privacy to location protection has been investigated in several recent papers. The definition of geo-indistinguishability [48] formalizes the notion of protecting a user's location within a radius r with a level of privacy that depends on r. The level of privacy is achieved by adding controlled random noise to the user's location. Bordenabe et al. [49] showed that, given a desired degree of geo-indistinguishability, it is possible to construct a mechanism that minimizes service quality loss using linear programming techniques.

However, Kifer et al. [50] showed that differential privacy will only erase the evidence of a single individual's private value when the individuals in the data are independent. This means there is potential for privacy leaks when the individuals' private values are correlated, as discussed by Olteanu et al. [51].

Generally speaking, obfuscation schemes will sacrifice the user's utility. While there is always a tradeoff between utility and privacy, there are some special cases. For example, Soma et al. [52] investigated location privacy protection in trip planning (TP) queries. They designed a method to protect location privacy by sending a false or cloaked location to the service provider that still yielded exact results for the TP queries. In this case, obfuscation is a good choice for privacy protection as there is no performance degradation.

2.4 Reducing Location Information Sharing

2.4.1 Caching

Cache systems have been proposed as a way to improve user privacy. In these systems, the POI data are prefetched and stored in cache before arriving at an area [53]. However, this means a huge amount of service data needs to be stored. MobiCrowd [54] preserves user privacy by querying neighbors for service data before sending the query to the LBS server, but if neighboring users cannot provide the answers, the query is sent to the LBS server and is still at risk. Zhu et al. [55] proposed the MobiCache scheme which attempts to cache additional data that has not yet been cached. However, it does not consider side information, which may be used by an adversary to infer the real location of users. Niu et al. [56] proposed a privacy metric to model the effect of caching. Their cache-aware dummy selection algorithms carefully combine k-anonymity, caching, and side information to achieve a higher privacy degree and caching hit ratio. But cooperation among community members is still required. Liu et al. [57] proposed a framework that enhances the privacy of LBS in wireless vehicular network scenarios through active caching.

2.4.2 Game Theory

Alternatively, a game theory approach can be used to reduce location information sharing. For example, Liu et al. [58] proposed a framework that enhances the location privacy of MCS applications by reducing the bidding and assignment steps in the MCS cycle.

2.5 Comparisons and Discussions

2.5.1 LPPMs Versus Other Privacy Preservation Techniques

Just as location privacy is a subcategory of data privacy, LPPM is a subcategory of privacy preservation techniques. On the one hand, the ideas behind most LPPMs are derived from generic privacy protection techniques. For example, obfuscation can be used to disguise other types of data, such as figures, and cryptography can be applied to any information. But, on the other hand, most LPPMs need to be modified to suit the particular characteristics of location data. A typical example is the notion of geo-indistinguishability [48], which associates a level of privacy with a radius r from the user's location according to a generic differential privacy definition. Additionally, special attention needs to be paid to the ability of location data to reveal connections between different information as stated in Sect. 1.2.4. In fact, a context linking attack is one of the most important research issues for many existing LPPMs, as can be seen in Table 2.1.

Table 2.1 Comparison of location privacy preservation mechanisms by adversary and attack models

Location privacy		Adversary and attack			
Preservation mechanism		Information obtain	Knowledge	Attack method	Target
Cryptography-based	PIR [4]	Col./Eav.	Obs./Con.	Con./Pro.	Identity/position
Anonymization	k-anonymity [7]	Col./Eav.	Observed	NC†	Identity (non-consistent)
	Distributed k-anonymity [12, 14]	Col./Eav./Com.	Obs./Con.	Con./Collusion	Identity (non-consistent)
	l-diversity [16]	Collecting	Obs./Con.	Context linking	Identity (non-consistent)
	Historical k-anonymity [18]	Collecting	Obs./Con.	Context linking	Identity (consistent)
	Mix-zone [21]	Collecting	Obs./Con.	Context linking	Identity (consistent)
	Mix-zone with road networks [20, 23]	Collecting	Obs./Con.	Context linking	Identity (consistent)
	Trajectory mix-zone [24]	Collecting	Obs./Con.	Context linking	Identity (consistent)
Obfuscation	Dummy locations [33]	Collecting	Observed	NC	Position
	Realistic dummies [36, 38, 39]	Collecting	Obs./Con.	Context linking	Position
	Dummy trajectories [34]	Collecting	Obs./Con.	Context linking	Position/Time
	Spatial obfuscation [41]	Collecting	Observed	Context linking	Position
	Obfuscation to road networks [46]	Collecting	Obs./Con.	Context linking	Position
	Obfuscation to correlated locations [47]	Collecting	Obs./Con.	Con./Pro.	Position
	Time obfuscation [43]	Collecting	Observed	Context linking	Time
	Spatiotemporal obfuscation [44]	Collecting	Obs./Con.	Context linking	Position/Time
	Geo-indistinguishable [48]	Collecting	Observed	Probability	Position
Reducing location sharing	Caching [56, 57]	Col./Eav./Com.	Obs./Pre./Con.	NC	Identity/position/time
	Game theory [58]	Col./Eav./Com.	Obs./Pre./Con.	NC	Identity/position/time

† NC: Not specified
* Col.: Collecting; Eav.: Eavesdropping; Com.: Compromising
$ Con.: Context linking; Pro.: Probability; Col.: Collusion
£ Obs.: Observed; Con.: Context; Pre.: Precise.

Table 2.2 Comparison of location privacy preservation mechanisms by TTP and metrics

Location privacy preservation mechanism		TTP required	Location privacy metric
Cryptography-based	PIR [4]	No	Certainty
Anonymization	Mix-zone [21]	Yes	Certainty
	k-anonymity [7]	Yes	Certainty
Obfuscation	Dummy locations [33]	No	Correctness
	Spatial obfuscation [41]	No	Correctness
	Temporal obfuscation [43]	No	Correctness
	Spatiotemporal obfuscation [45]	No	Correctness
	Geo-indistinguishable [48]	No	Geo-Indistinguishability
Reducing location sharing	Caching [56]	No	Information gain or loss
	Game theory [58]	No	Information gain or loss

2.5.2   Comparisons of the Four Different Groups

LPPMs are differentiated by their basic ideas. Cryptography schemes lower the risk of an adversary obtaining information. Anonymization breaks the links between identities and locations to make the information worthless. Obfuscation blurs the information to reduce the risk of disclosure. And reducing the amount of location sharing reduces the amount of information generated and transmitted through the whole system.

Additionally, each approach considers different types of adversaries and the attacks they perpetrate. Obfuscation schemes focus on spatial and temporal information, whereas anonymization emphasizes identity protection, while cryptography and reducing location sharing protect all three attributes of location information. An overall comparison is listed in Table 2.1.

Finally, anonymization schemes differ from the three other groups in two further ways. First, the anonymization is usually entrusted to a third party, as shown in Table 2.2. Second, these approaches require user cooperation to achieve their goals.

Despite these differences among the LPPMs, it is important to emphasize that they are not mutually exclusive. It is common to combine different techniques by first trying to reduce any unnecessary information sharing and then protecting the remaining transmissions with encryption. Anonymization is often used to protect identity information, and obfuscation is used to protect position/time information.

2.6 Performance Evaluation: Location Privacy Metrics

Comparing the performance of different LPPMs is highly dependent on the ability to quantify location privacy. However, there is not yet a standard for evaluating privacy. Indeed, it is rare for even two different research projects to use the same method of quantification [59].

Wagner et al. [60] provide a very detailed summary of privacy metrics, including many metrics that are not even in the scope of location privacy. Shokri et al. [1] argue that location privacy metrics should consider three key aspects: accuracy, uncertainty, and correctness. In this section, we reorganize the existing metrics into five categories.

2.6.1 Certainty

Certainty or uncertainty metrics are used to measure the ambiguity of an adversary with respect to finding a unique answer. This answer could be an identity or any other spatial or temporal information about the location.

2.6.1.1 Numerical Metrics

Duckham et al. [61] define the "level of privacy" as the number of different location coordinates sent by a user with a single location-based query. More points mean more ambiguity and, hence, a higher privacy level. The goal of their system is to be as ambiguous as possible while still getting the right answer for a POI query.

In the k-anonymity group of LPPMs, k is used to represent the level of privacy [7]. Similarly, p is used in p-sensitivity [15], and l is used in l-diversity [16].

2.6.1.2 Entropy-Based Metrics

Shannon entropy is the basis for many metrics. In location privacy, entropy-based metrics are computed based on the posterior probability of the adversary's estimates $\hat{x}$ based on his observations o:

$$\sum_{\hat{x}} Pr(\hat{x}|o) \log \frac{1}{Pr(\hat{x}|o)}. \tag{2.1}$$

Actually, numerical metrics can easily be converted into entropy-based metrics. For example, in a k-anonymity system, the equivalent entropy is

$$\sum_{k} \frac{1}{k} \log \frac{1}{1/k}. \tag{2.2}$$

The resulting value can be used to measure how well an adversary can identify a specific user in an anonymity set and disclose their position.

Entropy has also been used in cases where privacy is measured at more than one point in time. For example, in scenarios where the adversary tracks users over a period of time, entropy is computed at every point in time and the underlying probabilities are updated after each time stamp using Bayesian belief tables [62]. This approach accounts for the prior knowledge that the adversary acquired during previous time stamps once the first time stamp has been calculated.

The disadvantage of certainty metrics is that they do not take the correctness of the adversary's estimates into account because the true position x is not considered in the equation. This might be problematic. For example, if two positions are very close to each other, the locations may be revealed despite high entropy [63].

2.6.2   Correctness

2.6.2.1   Adversarial Success Rates

This metric measures the probability that an adversary will be successful, or the percentage of successes in a large number of attempts. Depending on the application scenario, success can be defined in different ways. For example, to evaluate the performance of an inference attack, Li et al.'s [64] successful rate is based on the success of inferring the correct demographics.

2.6.2.2   Distance-Based Metrics

Distance-based metrics quantify the error or expected distance between the true information and the estimated information, using any distance metric $d()$. A distance metric for a single location can be computed by the posterior probability of the adversary's estimate $\hat{x}$ based on their observations o, while the true position is x:

$$\sum_{\hat{x}} Pr(\hat{x}|o)d(x,\hat{x}). \tag{2.3}$$

And this can be extended to a trajectory by summation over multiple time stamps [63].

2.6.3   Information Gain or Loss

Information gain or loss metrics measure the amount of information that an adversary can possibly gain. They assume that privacy is higher when an adversary can gain less information. Similar to uncertainty metrics, many information gain metrics found their roots in numerical metrics or entropy-based metrics.

For example, Liu et al. [57] define the "privacy degree" as the percentage of queries that cached content can respond to as opposed to the service provider. As the cached content is in local memory, it is more secure than the LBS server.

Similarly, the number of packages uploaded by participants in MCS applications can also be used to measure privacy levels [58].

2.6.4 Geo-Indistinguishability

In statistical databases, differential privacy guarantees that any disclosure is equally likely regardless of whether or not an item is in the database [65]. In the context of location privacy, Andres et al. [48] proposed a useful term "geo-indistinguishability" to measure the level of privacy.

Definition 2.1 (ϵ-*geo-indistinguishability*): For each true location $x \in \mathscr{X}$, a mechanism $\mathscr{K}$ is a probabilistic function assigned to x as a probability distribution of $\mathscr{Z}$. And $Pr(\mathscr{K}(x) = z), z \in \mathscr{Z}$ is the probability that z is the location generated by $\mathscr{K}$ from x. Then, the *geo-indistinguishable level* of $\mathscr{K}$ is defined as:

$$GIL(\mathscr{K}, x, x') = \sup_{z \in \mathscr{Z}} \left| \ln \frac{Pr(\mathscr{K}(x) = z)}{Pr(\mathscr{K}(x') = z)} \right|$$
$$= \sup_{z \in \mathscr{Z}} \left| \ln \frac{Pr(z|x)}{Pr(z|x')} \right|, \tag{2.4}$$

where we use $Pr(z|x)$ instead of $Pr(\mathscr{K}(x) = z)$ for simplicity.

We say $\mathscr{K}$ satisfies ϵ-geo-indistinguishability if and only if, for all $x, x' \in \mathscr{X}$ and $z \in \mathscr{Z}$:

$$GIL(\mathscr{K}, x, x') \le \epsilon d_2(x, x'), \tag{2.5}$$

where $d_2(x, x')$ is the Euclidean distance between locations. Note that for all points x' within a radius of r from x, the definition forces the corresponding probabilities of generating the same released location z to be ϵr distant at most.

Therefore, the parameter ϵ represents the level of geo-indistinguishability.

2.6.5 Time

Time-based metrics focus on time as a resource that an adversary needs to spend to compromise a user's privacy. In some location privacy issues, the adversary aims to not only break privacy at a single time point, but also to track a target's location over time. For example, the adversary's tracking ability is measured by the maximum tracking time in [66], which is defined as the cumulative time that the size of the target's anonymity set remains 1.

This metric tends to overestimate a target's privacy because it assumes that the adversary has to be completely certain. To avoid the overestimation of privacy, the mean time to confusion measures the time during which the adversary's uncertainty stays below a confusion threshold [67].

2.6.6 Discussion on Performance Metrics

The metrics discussed above are the most frequently used in current research endeavors. However, there are some other ones. For instance, Shokri et al. [1] mention an *accuracy* metric, which is used to quantify the accuracy of the adversary's estimation. However, this metric it is not used very often as it does not reflect the certainty or the correctness of the results.

Although we used the correctness metric for our comparison, it is important to emphasize that different groups of LPPMs should use different metrics as they have different protection targets and methodologies. As such, evaluating the differences between LPPMs without considering specific contexts and goals is a relatively arbitrary exercise. Table 2.2 summarizes the most commonly used metrics for a selection of LPPMs for the interest of readers.

References

1. R. Shokri, G. Theodorakopoulos, J.-Y. Le Boudec, J.-P. Hubaux, Quantifying location privacy, in *Proceedings of the IEEE Symposium on Security and Privacy* (2011), pp. 247–262
2. B. Liu, W. Zhou, T. Zhu, L. Gao, Y. Xiang, Location privacy and its applications: a systematic study, in *IEEE Access*, vol. 6 (2018), pp. 17606–17624
3. S. Mascetti, D. Freni, C. Bettini, X.S. Wang, S. Jajodia, Privacy in geo-social networks: proximity notification with untrusted service providers and curious buddies. VLDB J. Int. J. Very Large Data. Bases **20**(4), 541–566 (2011)
4. G. Ghinita, P. Kalnis, A. Khoshgozaran, C. Shahabi, K.-L. Tan, Private queries in location based services: anonymizers are not necessary, in *Proceedings of ther ACM SIGMOD* (2008), pp. 121–132
5. G.F. Marias, C. Delakouridis, L. Kazatzopoulos, P. Georgiadis, Location privacy through secret sharing techniques, in *Proceedings of the IEEE International Symposium on a World of Wireless Mobile and Multimedia Networks* (IEEE, 2005), pp. 614–620
6. P. Chen, Y. Lin, W. Zhang, X. Li, S. Zhang, Preserving location and content privacy for secure ranked queries in location based services, in *Proceedings of the IEEE Trustcom/BigDataSE/ISPA* (IEEE, 2016), pp. 892–899
7. M. Gruteser, D. Grunwald, Anonymous usage of location-based services through spatial and temporal cloaking, in *Proceedings of the ACM MobiSys* (2003), pp. 31–42

8. B. Gedik, L. Liu, Location privacy in mobile systems: a personalized anonymization model, in *Proceedings of the IEEE ICDCS* (2005), pp. 620–629
9. T. Xu, Y. Cai, Exploring historical location data for anonymity preservation in location-based services, in *Proceedings of the IEEE INFOCOM* (2008)
10. Z. Huo, Y. Huang, X. Meng, History trajectory privacy-preserving through graph partition, in *Proceedings of the ACM Workshop on Mobile Location-Based Service* (2011), pp. 71–78
11. C. Bettini, S. Mascetti, X.S. Wang, D. Freni, S. Jajodia, Anonymity and historical-anonymity in location-based services, in *Privacy in Location-Based Applications* (Springer, Berlin, 2009), pp. 1–30
12. G. Zhong, U. Hengartner, A distributed k-anonymity protocol for location privacy, in *Proceedings of the IEEE PerCom* (2009), pp. 1–10
13. J. Li, H. Yan, Z. Liu, X. Chen, X. Huang, D.S. Wong, Location-sharing systems with enhanced privacy in mobile online social networks. IEEE Syst. J. **11**(2), 439–448 (2017)
14. C.-Y. Chow, M.F. Mokbel, X. Liu, Spatial cloaking for anonymous location-based services in mobile peer-to-peer environments. GeoInformatica **15**(2), 351–380 (2011)
15. A. Solanas, F. Sebé, J. Domingo-Ferrer, Micro-aggregation-based heuristics for p-sensitive k-anonymity: one step beyond, in *Proceedings of the ACM International Workshop on Privacy and Anonymity in Information Society* (2008), pp. 61–69
16. A. Machanavajjhala, D. Kifer, J. Gehrke, M. Venkitasubramaniam, l-diversity: privacy beyond k-anonymity. ACM Trans. Knowl. Discov. Data (TKDD) **1**(1), 3 (2007)
17. B. Bamba, L. Liu, P. Pesti, T. Wang, Supporting anonymous location queries in mobile environments with privacygrid, in *Proceedings of the ACM International Conference on World Wide Web* (2008), pp. 237–246
18. S. Mascetti, C. Bettini, X.S. Wang, D. Freni, S. Jajodia, Providenthider: an algorithm to preserve historical k-anonymity in LBS, in *Proceedings of the IEEE International Conference on Mobile Data Management: Systems, Services and Middleware* (2009), pp. 172–181
19. J. Krumm, Inference attacks on location tracks, in *Proceeding of the IEEE Percom* (2007), pp. 127–143
20. B. Palanisamy, L. Liu, Attack-resilient mix-zones over road networks: architecture and algorithms. IEEE Trans. Mob. Comput. **14**(3), 495–508 (2015)
21. A.R. Beresford, F. Stajano, Location privacy in pervasive computing. IEEE Pervasive Comput. **2**(1), 46–55 (2003)
22. B. Ying, D. Makrakis, H.T. Mouftah, Dynamic mix-zone for location privacy in vehicular networks. IEEE Commun. Lett. **17**(8), 1524–1527 (2013)
23. R. Lu, X. Lin, T.H. Luan, X. Liang, X. Shen, Pseudonym changing at social spots: an effective strategy for location privacy in vanets. IEEE Trans. Veh. Technol. **61**(1), 86–96 (2012)
24. S. Gao, J. Ma, W. Shi, G. Zhan, C. Sun, TrPF: a trajectory privacy-preserving framework for participatory sensing. IEEE Trans. Inf. Forensics Secur. **8**(6), 874–887 (2013)
25. Z. Xu, H. Zhang, X. Yu, Multiple mix-zones deployment for continuous location privacy protection, in *Proceedings of the IEEE Trustcom/BigDataSE/ISPA* (IEEE, 2016), pp. 760–766
26. J. Freudiger, M.H. Manshaei, J.-P. Hubaux, D.C. Parkes, Non-cooperative location privacy. IEEE Trans. Dependable Secur. Comput. **10**(2), 84–98 (2013)
27. X. Gong, X. Chen, K. Xing, D.-H. Shin, M. Zhang, J. Zhang, From social group utility maximization to personalized location privacy in mobile networks. IEEE/ACM Trans. Netw. (2017)
28. D. Yang, X. Fang, G. Xue, Truthful incentive mechanisms for k-anonymity location privacy, in *Proceedings of the IEEE INFOCOM* (2013), pp. 2994–3002
29. X. Gong, X. Chen, K. Xing, D.-H. Shin, M. Zhang, J. Zhang, Personalized location privacy in mobile networks: a social group utility approach, in *Proceedings of the IEEE INFOCOM* (2015), pp. 1008–1016
30. K. Chatzikokolakis, C. Palamidessi, A. Pazii, Methods for location privacy: a comparative overview (2016)
31. G. Ghinita, Privacy for location-based services. Synth. Lect. Inf. Secur. Priv. Trust **4**(1), 1–85 (2013)

32. S. Zhang, Q. Liu, G. Wang, Enhancing location privacy through user-defined grid in location-based services, in *Proceedings of the IEEE Trustcom/BigDataSE/ISPA* (IEEE, 2016), pp. 730–736
33. H. Kido, Y. Yanagisawa, T. Satoh, An anonymous communication technique using dummies for location-based services, in *Proceedings of the IEEE ICPS* (2005), pp. 88–97
34. T.-H. You, W.-C. Peng, W.-C. Lee, Protecting moving trajectories with dummies, in *Proceedings of the IEEE International Conference on Mobile Data Management* (2007), pp. 278–282
35. P.-R. Lei, W.-C. Peng, I.-J. Su, C.-P. Chang, Dummy-based schemes for protecting movement trajectories. J. Inf. Sci. Eng. **28**(2), 335–350 (2012)
36. J. Krumm, Realistic driving trips for location privacy, in *Proceedings of the IEEE PerCom* (2009), pp. 25–41
37. R. Chow, P. Golle, Faking contextual data for fun, profit, and privacy, in *Proceedings of the ACM workshop on Privacy in the Electronic Society* (ACM, 2009), pp. 105–108
38. H.J. Do, Y.-S. Jeong, H.-J. Choi, K. Kim, Another dummy generation technique in location-based services, in *Proceedings of the IEEE International Conference on Big Data and Smart Computing (BigComp)* (IEEE, 2016), pp. 532–538
39. T. Hara, A. Suzuki, M. Iwata, Y. Arase, X. Xie, Dummy-based user location anonymization under real-world constraints. IEEE Access **4**, 673–687 (2016)
40. C.A. Ardagna, M. Cremonini, E. Damiani, S.D.C. Di Vimercati, P. Samarati, Location privacy protection through obfuscation-based techniques, in *Proceedings of the IFIP Annual Conference on Data and Applications Security and Privacy* (Springer, 2007), pp. 47–60
41. C.A. Ardagna, M. Cremonini, S.D.C. di Vimercati, P. Samarati, An obfuscation-based approach for protecting location privacy. IEEE Trans. Dependable Secur. Comput. **8**(1), 13–27 (2011)
42. A. Gutscher, Coordinate transformation-a solution for the privacy problem of location based services? in *Proceedings of the IEEE International Parallel & Distributed Processing Symposium* (2006), pp. 7–13
43. R.-H. Hwang, Y.-L. Hsueh, H.-W. Chung, A novel time-obfuscated algorithm for trajectory privacy protection. IEEE Trans. Serv. Comput. **7**(2), 126–139 (2014)
44. M. Terrovitis, N. Mamoulis, Privacy preservation in the publication of trajectories, in *Proceedings of the IEEE International Conference on Mobile Data Management* (2008), pp. 65–72
45. G. Ghinita, M.L. Damiani, C. Silvestri, E. Bertino, Preventing velocity-based linkage attacks in location-aware applications, in *Proceedings of the ACM SIGSPATIAL International Conference on Advances in Geographic Information Systems* (2009), pp. 246–255
46. M. Duckham, L. Kulik, A formal model of obfuscation and negotiation for location privacy, in *Proceedings of the IEEE PerCom* (2005), pp. 152–170
47. Y. Xiao, L. Xiong, Protecting locations with differential privacy under temporal correlations, in *Proceedings of the ACM SIGSAC Conference on Computer and Communications Security* (2015), pp. 1298–1309
48. M.E. Andrés, N.E. Bordenabe, K. Chatzikokolakis, C. Palamidessi, Geo-indistinguishability: Differential privacy for location-based systems, in *Proceedings of the ACM SIGSAC Conference on Computer & Communications Security* (2013), pp. 901–914
49. N.E. Bordenabe, K. Chatzikokolakis, C. Palamidessi, Optimal geo-indistinguishable mechanisms for location privacy, in *Proceedings of the ACM SIGSAC Conference on Computer and Communications Security* (2014), pp. 251–262
50. D. Kifer, A. Machanavajjhala, No free lunch in data privacy, in *Proceedings of the ACM SIGMOD International Conference on Management of Data* (2011), pp. 193–204
51. A.-M. Olteanu, K. Huguenin, R. Shokri, M. Humbert, J.-P. Hubaux, Quantifying interdependent privacy risks with location data. IEEE Trans. Mob. Comput. **16**(3), 829–842 (2017)
52. S.C. Soma, T. Hashem, M.A. Cheema, S. Samrose, Trip planning queries with location privacy in spatial databases. World Wide Web **20**(2), 205–236 (2017)
53. S. Amini, J. Lindqvist, J. Hong, J. Lin, E. Toch, N.S. Cache, Cache: caching location-enhanced content to improve user privacy, in *Proceedings of the IEEE Mobisys* (2011)
54. R. Shokri, G. Theodorakopoulos, P. Papadimitratos, E. Kazemi, J.-P. Hubaux, Hiding in the mobile crowd: locationprivacy through collaboration. IEEE Trans. Dependable Secur. Comput. **11**(3), 266–279 (2014)

55. X. Zhu, H. Chi, B. Niu, W. Zhang, Z. Li, H. Li, Mobicache: when k-anonymity meets cache, in *Proceedings of the IEEE Globecom* (2013), pp. 820–825
56. B. Niu, Q. Li, X. Zhu, G. Cao, H. Li, Enhancing privacy through caching in location-based services, in *Proceedings of the IEEE INFOCOM* (2015)
57. B. Liu, W. Zhou, T. Zhu, L. Gao, T.H. Luan, H. Zhou, Silence is golden: enhancing privacy of location-based services by content broadcasting and active caching in wireless vehicular networks. IEEE Trans. Veh. Technol. **65**(12), 9942–9953 (2016)
58. B. Liu, W. Zhou, T. Zhu, H. Zhou, X. Lin, Invisible hand: a privacy preserving mobile crowd sensing framework based on economic models. IEEE Trans. Veh. Technol. (2016)
59. X. Zhang, X. Gui, F. Tian, A framework for measuring query privacy in location-based service. KSII Trans. Internet Inf. Syst. (TIIS) **9**(5), 1717–1732 (2015)
60. I. Wagner, D. Eckhoff, Technical privacy metrics: a systematic survey, http://arxiv.org/abs/1512.00327
61. M. Duckham, L. Kulik, Simulation of obfuscation and negotiation for location privacy, in *International Conference on Spatial Information Theory* (Springer, Berlin, 2005), pp. 31–48
62. Z. Ma, F. Kargl, M. Weber, Measuring long-term location privacy in vehicular communication systems. Comput. Commun. **33**(12), 1414–1427 (2010)
63. B. Hoh, M. Gruteser, Protecting location privacy through path confusion, in *Proceedings of the IEEE SecureComm* (2005), pp. 194–205
64. H. Li, H. Zhu, S. Du, X. Liang, X. Shen, Privacy leakage of location sharing in mobile social networks: attacks and defense. IEEE Trans. Dependable Secur. Comput. **1**, 1–1 (2016)
65. C. Dwork, Differential privacy: a survey of results, in *Proceedings of the International Conference on Theory and Applications of Models of Computation* (Springer, Berlin, 2008), pp. 1–19
66. M. Li, R. Poovendran, K. Sampigethaya, L. Huang, CARAVAN: providing location privacy for VANET, in *Proceedings of the Embedded Security in Cars (ESCAR) Workshop*, vol. 2 (2005), pp. 13–15
67. B. Hoh, M. Gruteser, H. Xiong, A. Alrabady, Preserving privacy in GPS traces via uncertainty-aware path cloaking, in *Proceedings of the ACM Conference on Computer and Communications Security* (2007), pp. 161–171

Chapter 3
Location Privacy in Mobile Social Network Applications

Location privacy has drawn much attention among mobile social network users, as the geo-location information can be used by the adversaries to launch localization attacks which focus on finding people's sensitive locations such as home and office place. In this chapter, we propose a community-based information sharing scheme to help the users to protect their home locations [1]. First, we study the existing home location prediction algorithms and conclude that they are all mainly based on the spatial and temporal features of the check-in data. Then we design the community-based information sharing scheme which aggregates the check-ins of all community members, thus change the overall spatial and temporal features. Finally, our simulation results validate that our proposed scheme greatly reduces the home location prediction accuracy and therefore can protect the user's privacy effectively.

The reminder of the chapter is organized as follows. Section 3.1 gives an brief introduction of the research background. Section 3.2 describes the existing sensitive location prediction methods in MSNs, as well as the adversary model and privacy metrics. The proposed community-based important location prediction scheme is described and analyzed in Sect. 3.3, along with detailed performance analysis and extensive numerical simulations. Finally, Sect. 3.4 gives the conclusion about this chapter.

3.1 Introduction

Location information is introduced into a variety of social network platforms to enrich people's interactivity and relationship. Many people like to share activities (check-ins), thoughts (tweets, status updates, etc.), pictures, videos, or interesting articles with friends, family, and the public. These shared posts often come along with location data (geo-tags). Although these information can be used to improve people's life quality, i.e., recommending famous place of interests to friends, they poses high privacy risks at the same time.

© The Author(s), under exclusive licence to Springer Nature Singapore Pte Ltd. 2018   33
B. Liu et al., *Location Privacy in Mobile Applications*,
SpringerBriefs on Cyber Security Systems and Networks,
https://doi.org/10.1007/978-981-13-1705-7_3

The geo-location information can be used by the adversaries to launch localization attacks which focus on finding people's position and time information. A type of dangerous attack aims to find important locations such as home and workplaces. There have been a number of papers investigating the home location identification problem, based on either the content of the posts [2] or the geo-tags in the check-ins [3]. And the research shows that the identification accuracy might be over 90% in many cases.

On the contrary, the research targeting on protecting sensitivity locations has been very rare. As an effort to fill this technique gap, we propose a community-based home location protection scheme in this paper. Our idea is based on the fact that people sometimes only need to share precise information with certain communities, such as colleagues, family members, or classmates. Therefore, when a user posts a check-in or tweets with the geo-tag, he/she can select to post this information as a member of a community which he/she belongs to. Then for the outside adversaries, the geo-location information becomes indistinguishable among the community members.

3.2 Sensitive Location Prediction by Users Social Network Data

Home location identification focuses on identifying home location of users in social networks. There are two types of approaches within this scope: content-based approach and check-in-based approach.

3.2.1 Content-Based Approach

Content-based approach infers home location of users by extracting location information from texts like tweets in social networks. Cheng et al. [2] used a classifier to identify words in tweets with a strong local geo-scope, combining with a lattice-based neighborhood smoothing model for refining a user's location estimation. Chandra et al. [4] employed a probabilistic framework to estimate the city-level location of a Twitter user, based on the content of the tweets in their dialogues. Mahumd et al. [5] used an ensemble of statistical and heuristic classifiers to predict Twitter users' home locations based on their tweeting behavior and content of tweets. Li et al. [6] combined users' multiple microblogs and used them to identify the location.

3.2.2 Check-In-Based Approach

Check-in-based approach infers home location of users utilizing check-in data of users. Cho et al. [3] inferred the home location by discretizing the world into 25 by

25 Km cells and defining the home location as the average position of check-ins in the cell with the most check-ins. Li et al. [7] identified home locations of users in Twitter based on the model using signals observed from friends and venues identified in tweets. Pontes et al. [8] used a majority voting scheme which takes the most popular location of a user as the home location. Liu et al. [9] obtained the estimated home locations using a hierarchical clustering method to cluster check-ins at night.

Besides the content and check-in-based approach, other information can also be used in home location prediction. The precision of the content-based approaches is generally city-level, which is not as good as the check-in-based approaches. Because the location information in the content is often blur. Therefore, we will use check-in-based approach to test our scheme in this paper.

As all the check-in-based home location prediction methods are based on the features of users' check-in data, we will first conclude the check-in behavior of users in mobile social networks in this section. We will also briefly describe the two location prediction algorithms which will be used to test our proposed scheme. The adversary model and privacy metric are given as well, as the fundamental of the rest parts of the paper.

3.2.3 Check-In Behavior of Users in Mobile Social Networks

3.2.3.1 Spatial Features of Check-In Data

Cho. et al. [3] explored the distribution of the check-ins numbers as a function of the distance from home and observed that the distribution follows a power law with exponential cutoff, i.e.,

$$f(d) = d^{\alpha} e^{\beta}, \tag{3.1}$$

where d is the check-in distance from home. α and β are the parameters vary for different datasets.

And such a phenomenon exists in different datasets including Brightkite and Gowalla.

3.2.3.2 Temporal Features of Check-In Data

Besides the spatial feature, the check-in data also have temporal feature. For example, check-ins at night (shared from 8:00 p.m. to 7:59 a.m. every day) are most likely to happen at the home location, while check-ins during work hours (from 8:00 a.m. to 6:59 p.m. on weekdays) have high probability to be linked to the office location.

3.2.4 Home Location Prediction Algorithms

The above-mentioned spatial and temporal features of the check-ins are used to predict the home locations. Here we introduce two typical algorithms based on the number of check-ins and time stamp clusterings, respectively.

3.2.4.1 Home Prediction by the Number of Check-Ins

Scellato et al. [10] defined the home location as the average position of check-ins in the cell with the most check-ins (Algorithm 1). They first divide the whole area into cells $\{cell_0, cell_1, ..., cell_i, ...\}$. Then the predicted home location $l_{u,h} = avg(l_{cell_{max}})$ is the average position of check-in locations in the cell with the most number of check-ins $cell_{max}$. Manual inspection shows that this algorithm can infer home locations with 85% accuracy [3].

3.2.4.2 Home Prediction by Clustering Check-Ins Based on Time Stamps

Liu et al. [9] proposed a user home/office locations prediction algorithm by clustering check-ins shared at night and work hours, respectively (Algorithm 2). First, the check-ins during the nighttime of user u are divided into clusters $\{cluster_{u,0}, cluster_{u,1}, ..., cluster_{u,i}, ...\}$ by a hierarchical clustering method. Then a home candidate $r_{u,h,i} = (g, n)$ is calculated from each $cluster_{u,i}$, where g is the center of all the check-in locations in $cluster_{u,i}$, and n is the number of check-ins in the cluster. Finally, the home candidates' list $R_{u,h}$ is formed by $\{r_{u,h,0}, r_{u,h,1}, ..., r_{u,h,i}, ...\}$, descending by the number of check-ins in each cluster. They showed that for 98.3% of users, at least one of the first three home candidates $r_{u,h,i}, i = 1, 2, 3$ are within 2 Km of the user's true home location.

3.2.5 The Adversary and Attack Models

An adversary's aim in the location privacy ground is collecting location information and using it to gain benefits. Based on the two key factors of the location privacy, the adversary and his/her attack can be characterized by "how" they obtain the information, "how" the attack is launched, "what" the information they obtained (knowledge), and "what" is the target.

In this paper, we assume that the adversary obtains the information by collecting shared or published geo-location information (i.e., check-ins with time stamps). And the obtained location information is precise in the sense that it is not processed by any obfuscation schemes.

And the attack target is people's sensitive positions such as the home locations. The adversaries use data mining and machine learning tool (Algorithms 1 and 2) to launch the attack.

3.2.6 Privacy Metrics

We use the "correctness" metric [11] to measure the performance of the proposed scheme. It is a distance-based metrics quantifying the error or expected distance between the true and predicted location. For a single location, it can be computed by the posterior probability of the adversary's estimates x based on his observations o, while the true position is x_c, i.e.,

$$\sum_x Pr(x|o)d(x, x_c). \tag{3.2}$$

In the context of this paper, x is the predicted home location based on the observed check-ins o. $d(x, x_c)$ is the distance calculated by the coordinates.

3.3 Protecting Important Locations in Social Networks

3.3.1 Community-Based Geo-Location Information Sharing Scheme

Nowadays, many people use social networking apps and Web sites such as Facebook and Twitter to share their experiences and thoughts with other people, through posts along with geo-location data. As these location data are generally available to the public, they might be collected by adversaries and used to predict a user's home location.

On the other hand, people in social networks belong to different communities, and the communities are formed based on common features such as family members, similar interests, and classmates. Moreover, people may belong to multiple communities at the same time. For example, one may be in a community who graduate from the same university and another community who like to travel as well.

In reality, people sometimes only want to share precise information within certain communities. Based on this fact, we may enable the user to select to post this information as an individual or as a member of a community which he/she belongs to. The former case is the current scheme used in social networks. And the latter case can prevent possible outside adversaries from knowing the exact owner of the posts.

Figures 3.1 and 3.2 illustrate our idea of the community-based geo-location information sharing scheme. As shown in Fig. 3.1, the user "Luke Liu" posts a check-in

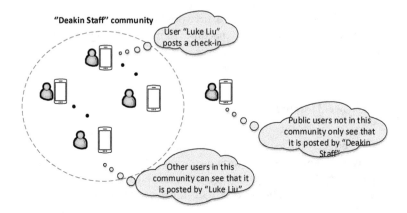

Fig. 3.1 Illustration of the community-based geo-location information sharing scheme

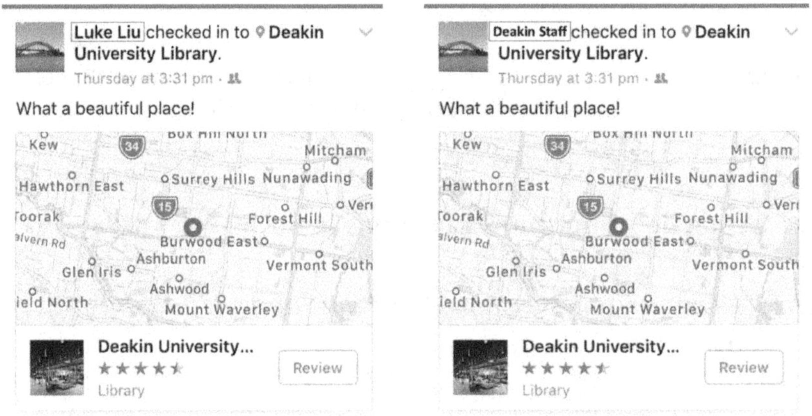

(a) Information seen by community members. (b) Information seen by people outside the community.

Fig. 3.2 Example of the community-based geo-location information sharing scheme

at a point of interest "Deakin University Library" as the member of "Deakin Staff" community, other users in this community can see that it is posted by "Luke Liu" (Fig. 3.2a), while public users who are not in this community only see that it is posted by a member of the "Deakin Staff" community (Fig. 3.2b).

3.3.2 Aggregated Check-In Behavior of Users in a Community

With this scheme, the geo-location data collected by the adversaries will be the aggregated information of different communities. We now investigate the aggregated check-in behavior of users and its impact on the prediction of home location.

As all the home location prediction algorithms are based on the spatial and temporal features of check-ins. The temporal feature is not changed by our scheme. Thus, we focus on the change of the spatial feature under our proposed community-based geo-location information sharing scheme.

Assuming that for each user, the distributions of check-in numbers as a function of the distance from home follow the Eq. (3.1). With the community-based geo-location information sharing scheme, all check-ins from the same community are indistinguishable for the outsiders. Therefore, we have

$$f_c(d) = \int_{d_{h-h}} f(|\mathbf{d} - \mathbf{d_{h-h}}|) \cdot f_{h-h}(d_{h-h}), \tag{3.3}$$

where $f_c()$ is distributions of check-in numbers in a community as a function of the distance from a certain user's home. f_{h-h} is the distribution of home distances between members in the same community.

Intuitively, traditional home location algorithms are based on the precondition that each user has "one" home location. When our scheme aggregates the check-ins in communities, it hides a single user's home among all home locations of the community.

3.3.3 Datasets and Evaluation Setup

We evaluate our scheme using the Gowalla dataset which is collected by the authors of [12] from Gowalla which was a popular LBSN service back in 2011. The dataset was collected from February 2009 to October 2010, and it contains 6,442,892 check-ins. Besides location information, the dataset also includes the corresponding social data which contain around 1.9 million users and 9.5 million edges. Due to the large data sparsity, we take the check-in data in New York as an example, as New York is among the areas with most check-ins (138957) in the dataset. In addition, we only focus on users who have conducted at least 100 check-ins in each city and we term these users as active users (241 in total).

As our proposed scheme is based on the community structure, community detection is the first step. Community detection methods have been investigated in many papers. It is closely related to the ideas of graph partitioning in graph theory and hierarchical clustering in sociology. According to the comparative analysis [13], among

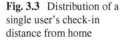

Fig. 3.3 Distribution of a single user's check-in distance from home

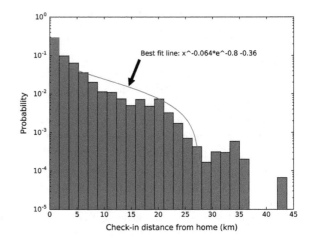

all the community detection algorithms, Infomap [14] has the best performance on undirected and unweighted graphs. Therefore, we use Infomap in this work.

The Gowalla dataset contains the links among users. To detect communities of u, we first find all his/her friends as well as the links among them. Then, we delete u and all edges linked to him and apply Infomap algorithm to the remaining part of the graph. The average community number of each active user in our simulation is 3.215, and the average community size is 14.727.

3.3.4 Impact on Spatial Feature of the Check-Ins

In order to validate that our proposed scheme can protect home location, we first verify that it indeed changes the spatial features of the check-in data. Figures 3.3 and 3.4 compare the check-in number distributions of a single user and a community. It can be seen that when calculated using the community's data, the curve becomes more flat. And when we fit the power law parameters using maximum likelihood, the parameters change a lot as well ($\alpha = -0.064$ vs -0.002, $\beta = -0.8$ vs 2.25).

3.3.5 Impact on Home Location Prediction Algorithms

Now we investigate the impact on the two different home location prediction algorithms.

Figure 3.5 gives an example (user id $= 1940$) of the home location prediction results using Algorithm 1. It shows that our scheme introduces big perturbations to the predicted home location.

Fig. 3.4 Distribution of a community's check-in distance from home

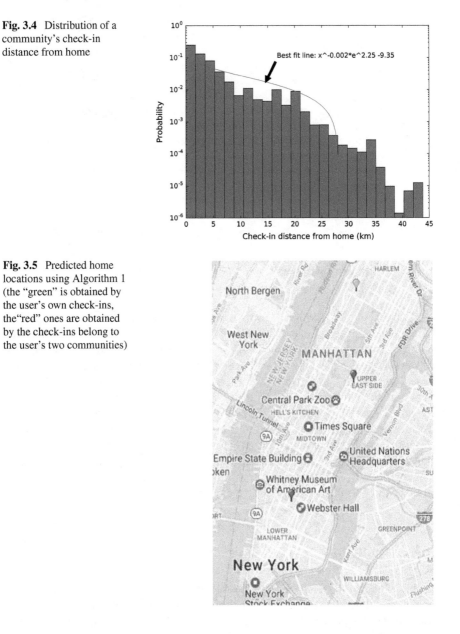

Fig. 3.5 Predicted home locations using Algorithm 1 (the "green" is obtained by the user's own check-ins, the "red" ones are obtained by the check-ins belong to the user's two communities)

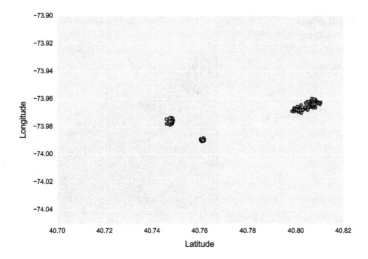

Fig. 3.6 Clustering of a single user's check-in data during nighttime

With regard to Algorithm 2, using the user's own or the communities' check-in data produces different clustering results, as shown in Figs. 3.6 and 3.7. Thus, the accuracy of the home location prediction is reduced accordingly, as shown in Fig. 3.8.

Finally, we calculate the correctness of home location prediction under our proposed community-based geo-location information sharing scheme, as shown in Figs. 3.9 and 3.10. As we do not have the true home locations of users, we use the prediction results using only the user's own check-ins as his/her "actual" home. The average correctness of Algorithm 1 is 1942 m, and the value for Algorithm 2 is 4345m. It validates that our proposed scheme brings great obfuscation for the location prediction algorithms. Moreover, the correctness of Algorithm 1 is averagely smaller because of the procedure of "discretizing." The impact of the cell size on the results will be further investigated in the future works.

3.4 Summary

In this paper, we have studied the location privacy issue in MSNs. We propose a community-based scheme to deal with the challenge of sensitive location protection. The effect of the proposed scheme on the features of the geo-location information is analyzed. Moreover, we setup an evaluation system and validate our proposed scheme against two existing home location prediction algorithms, on the real-life dataset. The simulation results show that the proposed scheme can effectively protect the MSN users' sensitive location privacy.

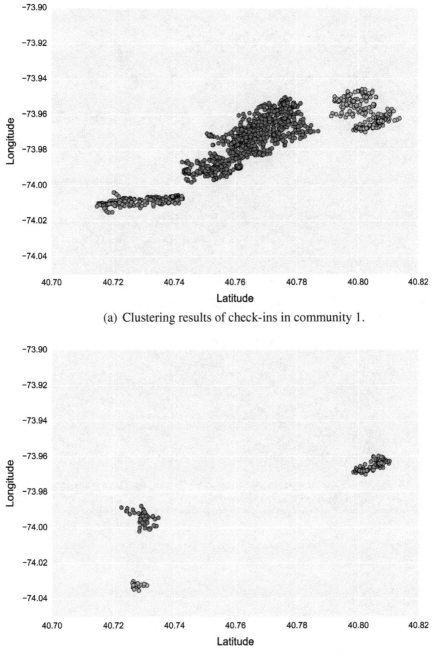

(a) Clustering results of check-ins in community 1.

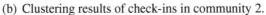

(b) Clustering results of check-ins in community 2.

Fig. 3.7 Clustering of communities' check-in data during nighttime

Fig. 3.8 Predicted home locations by Algorithm 2 (the "brown" ones are top three home location candidates obtained by the user's own check-ins, the "blue" ones are home location candidates obtained by the check-ins belong to the user's two communities)

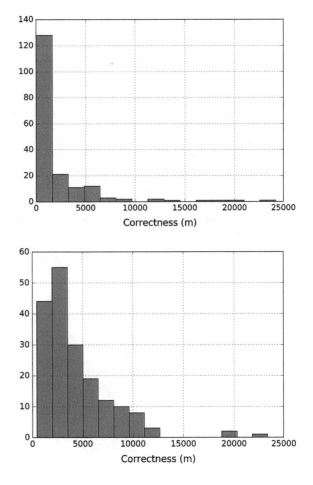

Fig. 3.9 Correctness of the home prediction results using Algorithm 1 under the community-based geo-location information sharing scheme

Fig. 3.10 Correctness of the home prediction results using Algorithm 2 under the community-based geo-location information sharing scheme

References

1. B. Liu, W. Zhou, S. Yu, K. Wang, Y. Wang, Y. Xiang, J. Li, Home location protection in mobile social networks: a community based method (short paper), in *International Conference on Information Security Practice and Experience* (Springer, Cham, 2017), pp. 694-704
2. Z. Cheng, J. Caverlee, K. Lee, You are where you tweet: a content-based approach to geo-locating twitter users, in *Proceedings ACM International Conference on Information and Knowledge Management* (2010), pp. 759–768
3. E. Cho, S.A. Myers, J. Leskovec, Friendship and mobility: user movement in location-based social networks, in *Proceedings of the ACM SIGKDD* (2011), pp. 1082–1090
4. S. Chandra, L. Khan, F.B. Muhaya, Estimating twitter user location using social interactions–a content based approach, in *Proceedings of the IEEE PASSAT* (2011), pp. 838–843
5. J. Mahmud, J. Nichols, C. Drews, Where is this tweet from? Inferring home locations of twitter users. ICWSM **12**, 511–514 (2012)
6. G. Li, J. Hu, J. Feng, K.-l. Tan, Effective location identification from microblogs, in *Proceedings of the ICDE* (2014), pp. 880–891

7. R. Li, S. Wang, H. Deng, R. Wang, K.C.-C. Chang, Towards social user profiling: unified and discriminative influence model for inferring home locations, in *Proceedings of the ACM SIGKDD* (2012), pp. 1023–1031

8. T. Pontes, M. Vasconcelos, J. Almeida, P. Kumaraguru, V. Almeida, We know where you live: privacy characterization of foursquare behavior, in *Proceedings of the ACM Conference on Ubiquitous Computing* (2012), pp. 898–905

9. H. Liu, Y. Zhang, Y. Zhou, D. Zhang, X. Fu, K. Ramakrishnan, Mining checkins from location-sharing services for client-independent IP geolocation, in *Proceedings of the IEEE INFOCOM* (2014), pp. 619–627

10. S. Scellato, A. Noulas, R. Lambiotte, C. Mascolo, Socio-spatial properties of online location-based social networks. ICWSM **11**, 329–336 (2011)

11. R. Shokri, G. Theodorakopoulos, J.-Y. Le Boudec, J.-P. Hubaux, Quantifying location privacy, in *Proceedings of the IEEE Security and Privacy* (2011), pp. 247–262

12. A. Clauset, M.E. Newman, C. Moore, Finding community structure in very large networks. Phys. Rev. E **70**(6), 066111 (2004)

13. A. Lancichinetti, S. Fortunato, Community detection algorithms: a comparative analysis. Phys. Rev. E **80**(5), 056117 (2009)

14. M. Rosvall, C.T. Bergstrom, Maps of random walks on complex networks reveal community structure. Natl. Acad. Sci. **105**(4), 1118–1123 (2008)

Chapter 4
Location Privacy in Mobile Crowd Sensing Applications

The privacy issue strongly impedes the development of mobile crowd sensing (MCS) applications. Under the current MCS framework, processes including bidding, task assignment, and sensed data uploading are all potentially risky for participants. As an effort toward this issue, we propose a framework which enhances the location privacy of MCS applications by reducing the bidding and assignment steps in the MCS cycle [1]. Meanwhile, to reduce the unnecessary privacy loss while maintaining the required quality of service, the economic theory is used to help both the service provider (SP) and participants to decide their strategies. We propose schemes based on both the Monopoly and Oligopoly models. In the former case, the participants cooperate to gain exclusive control of the supply of crowd sensing data, while the latter case is a state of limited competition. The parameters in different schemes are analyzed, and the strengths and weaknesses of both schemes are discussed. Additionally, the proposed schemes are evaluated by extensive simulations, and the results are discussed in detail.

The rest of the chapter is organized as follows. Section 4.1 gives a brief introduction of the research background. Section 4.2 introduces the system model and problem formulation. The details of our proposed privacy-preserving MCS framework is presented in Sect. 4.3. Section 4.4 gives the simulation results and performance analysis. Finally, Sect. 4.5 draws the conclusion about this chapter.

4.1 Introduction

Mobile crowd sensing (MCS) presents *"a new sensing paradigm that empowers ordinary citizens to contribute data sensed or generated from their mobile devices, aggregates and fuses the data in the cloud for crowd intelligence extraction and people-centric service delivery"* [2]. The term MCS [3] is now used to refer to a broad range of sensing paradigms including some other popular terms such as participatory sensing or opportunistic sensing.

© The Author(s), under exclusive licence to Springer Nature Singapore Pte Ltd. 2018   47
B. Liu et al., *Location Privacy in Mobile Applications*,
SpringerBriefs on Cyber Security Systems and Networks,
https://doi.org/10.1007/978-981-13-1705-7_4

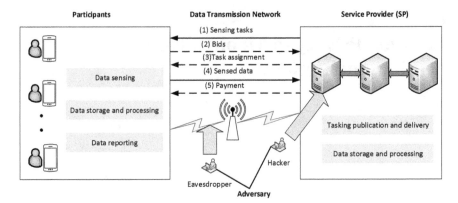

Fig. 4.1 System architecture of mobile crowd sensing applications

In recent years, there has been a wide range of new MCS applications, which can be mainly divided into two categories: the environment-centric applications and the people-centric applications. Examples of the former category include air quality monitoring projects—Common Sense [4] and Haze Watch [5], noise monitoring project—Ear-phone [6] and traffic monitoring projects—Car- Tel [7] and Nericell [8]. The people-centric applications include people health monitoring such as DietSense [9] and social information sharing like BikeNet [10].

An important aspect of MCS applications is the privacy threats when they potentially collect sensitive data pertaining to individuals. Specifically, the sensitive information such as people's locations or mobility traces may be revealed. Once participators realize the potentially personal information disclosure, they are unwilling to participate in the campaign and use the services. This will obviously degrade the quality of crowdsourced data and reduce the influence of the campaign as well as users' benefits. Therefore, how to ensure the participators' privacy is the most urgent task for the promotion of MCS applications.

To design better privacy-preserving methods for MCS applications, we need to consider the special features. As shown in Fig. 4.1, an MCS application generally consists of five steps: sensing task publication, bids submission, task assignment, uploading sensed data, and payment. This scheme is cost-effective, as the service provider (SP) could choose proper participants for each sensing task according to their bids. However, it has some weaknesses from the perspective of privacy. For example, if a participant submits a bid for a sensing task for information at location l at time t, it implies that he has been at that certain location at that certain time. Once the bid information is obtained by any adversary, the participant's location privacy is exposed even without uploading the actual data packet, and he loses privacy for nothing. On the other hand, some MCS applications do not have the bids process and participants upload all the data they have gathered to the server. This introduces duplications for the SP and unnecessary privacy loss as well. We need to reduce the redundancy while maintaining the SP's quality of service (QoS).

As motivated by the aforementioned issues, in this chapter, we develop a location privacy-preserving framework based on economic models for MCS applications. The proposed mechanism leaves out the bids and tasks' assignment processes which represent privacy risks to participants. Instead, the SP's requirement of QoS and participants' benefits are achieved under the law of supply and demand, i.e., the SP designs the incentives for the tasks to guarantee the expected QoS, while the participants try to maximize their benefits while considering the privacy costs.

4.2 System Model and Problem Formulation

4.2.1 The General Mobile Crowd Sensing System

We consider an air quality monitoring task which is performed via an MCS system illustrated in Fig. 4.1. The system consists of an SP, which has a central repository hosted on a cloud server, and many participants, each having a personal sensing device (PSD) which includes a mobile air quality sensor and a smartphone to upload the data via the data transmission network. At the beginning of each round of MCS task, the SP first broadcasts the task duration T, the *Region of Task* (RoT), and some other information like the budget. Then each participant from a set $\mathcal{P}$ who wishes to take part in the MCS task is required to upload some air quality data gathered by his PSD and will get a reward afterward according to the data he has uploaded. The sensed data consist of a series of data report d presented as $\langle l, t, AQI \rangle$, where l and t are the location and time stamp of d. AQI is the sensed air quality index.

Moreover, we assume that the whole RoT is partitioned into L discrete subregions (locations), representing by a set $\mathcal{L}$, and for one task duration T, time is presented by discrete stamps within the set of $\mathcal{T} = \{1, 2, \ldots, t, \ldots, T\}$. The location set of a participant during the T period is defined as $\mathcal{L}_{p,T} = \{l_{p,t} | \forall t \in T\}$.

Important symbols used in this subsection and following parts of the chapter are listed in Table 4.1 for reference.

4.2.2 The Basic Idea of Privacy-Preserving MCS Application Framework

For the MCS applications, we assume that there exist adversaries including eavesdroppers and hackers [11], as illustrated in Fig. 4.1. Specifically, an eavesdropper could capture the data traffic between the SP and participants via monitoring the communication channels, while a hacker could access and obtain all data in the SP. Therefore, to reduce the risk of privacy leakage, both the communications between the two parties and information stored in the SP should be reduced. For example, even if a participant only submits a bid for a sensing task for information at location l

Table 4.1 Summary of important symbols

$\mathscr{P}, \mathscr{L}, \mathscr{D}, \mathscr{T}$	The participants, distinct regions (locations), sensing data reports, and time stamp sets
P, L, D, T	The sizes of the participants, distinct regions (locations), sensing data reports, and time stamp sets
p, l, d, t	The elements of participants, distinct regions (locations), sensing data reports, and time stamp sets
AQI	The air quality index
s	The upload strategy of the participant with two possible values: upload (1) or not (0)
Q	The QoS of the MCS application
u	The utility of participant
LPL	The location privacy loss which is the difference between the location privacy degree before and after the MCS task
$H(p)$	The location privacy degree of the participant p
m	The payment from SP to the participants
q	The expected number of total uploaded packets in a certain location
q_i	The expected number of uploaded packets in a certain location by participant i
$m(q) = A - Bq$	$m(q)$ is the price when the total number of packets is q, in which A and B are parameters in the price function
c	The marginal costs of participants for each packet uploading
α	The weight factor of location privacy loss
β	The payment factor of the SP. Bigger β means the SP wishes to pay more to attract more participants for the task

at time t, it implies that he has been at that certain location at that certain time. Once the bid information is obtained by any adversary, the participant's location privacy is exposed even without uploading the actual data packet.

To achieve the goal, the processes of bidding and task allocation (see dash lines in Fig. 4.1) in traditional MCS schemes [12] are eliminated. Our new proposed MCS framework is like this: The budget of payment m_l for all reports which are collected at location l is published along with the sensing tasks at the first step. Then each participant decides his own upload strategy $s^{p,d}$, $d \in \mathscr{D}_p$ for all the data he has collected, according to the payment information published by the SP. The strategy $s^{p,d}$, $d \in \mathscr{D}_p$ has two possible values: upload (1) or not (0).

In this case, the location privacy of the participants can be improved. Because if a participant p sends a bid for data packet at location l, the adversary could know that l is in p's location set within the task duration T. On the contrary, our *no-bidding* framework reduces the risk.

4.2.3 Location Privacy Metric

In order to evaluate the privacy issue quantity, we need to define the metric for location privacy measurement. Entropy-based metrics [13] and distortion-based metrics [14] are two major ways to measure privacy, wherein entropy can be seen as the uncertainty in determining the real location of a user from all the candidates. As entropy has been widely used in the literature [13], we will also use it to measure the location privacy degree.

Definition 4.1 Location Privacy Degree (LPD):
For a participant's location information set $\mathcal{L}_{p,T} = \{l_{p,t}|\forall t \in T\}$, its privacy degree can be measured by the information entropy as follows:

$$H(p) = \sum_{l \in \mathcal{L}_{p,T}} Pr(x_l = l) \log_2 \frac{1}{Pr(x_l = l)}, \tag{4.1}$$

where x_l is guess of l from the adversary.

For example, if the adversary has no knowledge for an k-length location set, he/she has to guess from all the possible locations, then the privacy degree is

$$H(p) = kL\frac{1}{L} \log_2 \frac{1}{1/L} = k \log_2 L. \tag{4.2}$$

Therefore, the location privacy loss (LPL) of p during a MCS task is the difference between his LPDs at time 0 and T:

$$LPL_p = \sum_{r \in \mathcal{R}_p} [H_0(p) - H_T(p)] \tag{4.3}$$

$$= \sum_{t \in \mathcal{T}, l \in \mathcal{L}_{p,T}} s^{p,d\langle l,t,AQI\rangle} \log_2 L. \tag{4.4}$$

4.2.4 Economic Models for the MCS Application

As stated in Sect. 4.2.2, we eliminate the processes of bidding and task allocation. Therefore, we need to find a new way to help the SP to decide its payment and the participants to decide their upload strategy. Here we introduce economic models for the MCS application. We first draw an analogy between our application and the economic activity: The SP acts like a consumer who buys useful data packets from participants who can provide the needed outputs. The corresponding mathematical models are described in detail in the following part.

4.2.4.1 Service Provider Modeling

When considered as a consumer, the SP's satisfaction is decided by the QoS. In practice, the QoS, i.e., the accuracy of the air quality monitoring, depends on whether the SP can get the reports which have suitable temporal and spatial properties to cover the required areas with favorable frequency. We define the QoS at the location l, as the percentage of task durations during which the SP gets at least one data packet.

$$Q_l = \frac{\sum\limits_{1 \leq i \leq n_T} \left\lceil \sum\limits_{iT \leq t \leq (i+1)T} \sum\limits_{p \in \mathscr{P}} I(s^{p, d\langle l, t, AQI \rangle}, Y) \right\rceil_l^1}{n_T}, \tag{4.5}$$

where $\lceil x \rceil_l^1$ means the data reports for the same location l are calculated only once. And the overall QoS for all RoT is:

$$Q = \frac{\sum\limits_{l \in \mathscr{L}} Q_l}{L}. \tag{4.6}$$

In order to achieve the targeted Q_{th}, the SP has to pay incentives (e.g., a certain amount of money) to participants to encourage people to upload data.

4.2.4.2 Participants' Modeling

As the producer, a participant's target is the utility which is decided by the payment he could receive and the cost of the location privacy loss.

Now we can define the utility of p accordingly:

Definition 4.2 The utility of each participant p is

$$u_p = \sum\limits_{l \in \mathscr{L}} m_{l,p} - \alpha \cdot LPL_p, \tag{4.7}$$

where $m_{l,p}$ is the payment to p for uploading the report at location l, and α is the privacy weight factor.

4.2.4.3 Pricing Modeling

The connection between the SP and the participants' problems is the payment. When the payment from the SP is higher, more participants tend to upload their data, and the QoS can raise accordingly. Therefore, we use a pricing modeling to bridge the above two problems together.

As the value of packets at a given location l decreases with the number, we define the price as an inverse demand function:

$$m_l(q_l) = A - Bq_l,$$ (4.8)

where q_l is the number of uploaded packets, A and B are parameters.

Therefore, for the SP, we have

$$m_l = m_l(q_l) \times q_l.$$ (4.9)

And for the participants, we have

$$m_{l,p} = \begin{cases} m_l(q_l), & \text{if } s^{p,d\langle l,t,AirQuality\rangle} = 1 \\ 0, & \text{if } s^{p,d\langle l,t,AirQuality\rangle} = 0 \end{cases}$$ (4.10)

Finally,

$$q_l = \sum_{p \in \mathscr{P}, t \in \mathscr{T}} s^{p,d\langle l,t,AQI\rangle}.$$ (4.11)

4.2.5 Problem Formulation

Now we have set up the MCS framework based on economic models, so we can formulate the problem based on these models. Under the economic laws, both the consumer (i.e., the SP) and the producer (i.e., the participant) try to maximize their welfare. In order to achieve our privacy preservation target, we define the location privacy loss of the participant as his cost. Therefore, the participant's utility maximization problem can be defined as:

Problem 4.1 (*Participant Problem*)

$$\max \sum_{l \in \mathscr{L}} (m_{l,p} - \alpha \cdot LPL_{l,p}).$$ (4.12)

On the other hand, the SP would like to minimize the cost, its problem is to minimize total payment to the participants who upload the reports, with the satisfactory completion rate of the sensing tasks.

Problem 4.2 (*Service Provider Problem*)

$$\min \sum_{l \in \mathscr{L}} m_l$$ (4.13)

$$s.t. \ Q \geq Q_{th}.$$

Combining the above two problems, we have a multiobjective optimization problem:

$$\begin{cases} \min \sum_{l \in \mathscr{L}} m_l \\ \max \sum_{l \in \mathscr{L}} (m_{l,p} - \alpha \cdot LPL_{l,p}) \end{cases} \tag{4.14}$$

$$s.t. \ Q \geq Q_{th}$$
$$m_l = \sum_{p \in \mathscr{P}_l} m_{l,p}.$$

4.3 Privacy-Preserving MCS Schemes Based on Economic Models

The optimal solution of this constrained linear problem can be easily obtained on the condition that the SP could communicate with participants without obstacle and coordinate the uploading strategies of all participants. However, as mentioned in the previous section, the intercommunication between the SP and participants is reduced to protect the location privacy. Therefore, in this semi-blind market, we have to introduce the invisible hand of market principle to help to solve the problem. Specifically, to achieve maximum profits, participants may follow the Monopoly or Oligopoly strategy. We define the two cases as follows, respectively [15].

Definition 4.3 Monopoly case for participants: A Monopoly case is the situation in which we suppose that all participants in the MCS task are somehow able to collude and target to maximize the overall profit, which is then divided among them. Therefore, they *as a whole* have exclusive control of the supply of data packets in the MCS applications.

Definition 4.4 Oligopoly case for participants: A (Cournot's) Oligopoly case is the situation in which the participants are in a state of limited competition, each acting strategically, seeking to maximize *his own* profit given other participants' decisions.

In the rest part of this section, we will present two schemes based on two different cases described in Definitions 4.3 and 4.4 to solve the above problem.

4.3.1 The Monopoly Model-Based Scheme (MMBS)

First, we consider the Monopoly case. We have the following definitions and assumptions[1]:

- Participants' total output at a given location: q.
- Participant i's output at a given location: q_i.
- The constant marginal cost of participants for each packet upload (caused by location privacy loss): $c = \alpha \cdot LPL_p$.
- Inverse demand function: $m(q) = A - Bq$.

In our air quality monitoring application, the actual number of packets uploaded by a given participant at a given location is either 0 or 1. Therefore, we could use the upload probability instead. Let

$$Pr\{s^{i,d\langle l,t,AirQuality\rangle} = 1\} = q_i, \tag{4.15}$$

then we have

$$\mathbb{E}[s^{i,d\langle l,t,AirQuality\rangle}] = q_i, i \in [1, n], \tag{4.16}$$

and

$$\mathbb{E}\left[\sum_{p\in\mathscr{P}, t\in\mathscr{T}} s^{p,d\langle l,t,AQI\rangle}\right] = q. \tag{4.17}$$

4.3.1.1 Participants' Upload Strategy

Using the above assumptions, the overall benefit of all participants is defined as

$$u(s) = m(q) \times q - c \times q. \tag{4.18}$$

To find the value of q which maximizes the profit of participants, let

$$\frac{du}{dq} = \frac{dm(q)}{dq} \times q + m(q) - c. \tag{4.19}$$

From

$$\frac{du}{dq} = \frac{dm(q)}{dq} \times q + m(q) - c = 0, \tag{4.20}$$

---

[1]We assume that the model for each location l is the same. Thus, the subscript l is left out in the rest part of this section for simplicity, e.g., q can be seen as q_l, and LPL_p is used to present $LPL_{p,l}$.

substituting $m(q) = A - Bq$, we have

$$q = \frac{A - c}{2B}.$$

$$(4.21)$$

Assuming that there are total n participants who have the packet at location l, then

$$q_i = \frac{1}{n} \frac{A - c}{2B}, i \in [1, n].$$

$$(4.22)$$

4.3.1.2   SP's Pricing Strategy

Slightly different from traditional economic models, we let the SP define parameters A and B in the inverse demand function to guarantee the QoS. Assuming that the SP's targeted QoS is Q_{th} for all locations, then for a given area l, the probability of at least one participant has uploaded data should satisfy

$$P_r \left\{ \sum_{p \in \mathscr{P}, t \in \mathscr{T}} s^{p, d \langle l, t, AQI \rangle} \geq 1 \right\}$$

$$(4.23)$$

$$= 1 - \prod_{1 \leq i \leq n} (1 - q_i)$$

$$(4.24)$$

$$= 1 - (1 - q_i)^n \geq Q_{th},$$

$$(4.25)$$

therefore, the minimum value of q_i should satisfy

$$q_i = 1 - \sqrt[n]{1 - Q_{th}},$$

$$(4.26)$$

and

$$q = n(1 - \sqrt[n]{1 - Q_{th}}).$$

$$(4.27)$$

The total payment for each location l is

$$m = (A - Bq) \times q,$$

$$(4.28)$$

combining with the participants' strategies presented by Eq. (4.21), we have

$$A = \frac{2m}{q} - c,$$

$$(4.29)$$

and

$$B = \frac{A - c}{2q}.$$ (4.30)

Also we have the constraint that $A - c > 0$ which guarantees positive utility for the participants, thus

$$m > cq,$$ (4.31)

where cq is the lower bound of the SP's budget given the values of c and Q_{th}.
Thus, we can set

$$m = \beta cq,$$ (4.32)

where $\beta > 1$ is the SP's payment factor. Bigger β means the SP wishes to pay more to attract more participants for the task.

And the process of our proposed Monopoly model-based scheme is summarized in Algorithm 1.

Algorithm 1: Monopoly Model-Based Scheme (MMBS).

---

1 **Initialization:** Define the targeted QoS Q_{th}, and the participants' cost c.
2 *SP's Pricing Strategy*:
3 **for** $l \in \mathcal{L}$ **do**
4   Allocate the budget $m = \beta cq$, where $\beta > 1$ is the payment factor;
5   Find the expected number of participants n at location l under the budget m;
6   Calculate $q = n(1 - \sqrt[n]{1 - Q_{th}})$;
7   Defining pricing strategy:

$$m(q) = A - Bq,$$

    where

$$A = \frac{2m}{q} - c, \quad B = \frac{A - c}{2q}.$$

    Broadcast A, B and n to all participants.
8 **end**
9 *Participant i's upload strategy*:
10 **for** $l \in \mathcal{L}$ **do**
11   Calculate $q_i = \frac{1}{n}\frac{A-c}{2B}$;
12   Set the upload strategy which satisfies: $Pr\{s^{i,d\langle l,t,AirQuality\rangle} = 1\} = q_i$.
13 **end**

4.3.2   Cournot's Oligopoly Model-Based Scheme (COMBS)

Now we consider the Cournot's Oligopoly case in which the participants are not completely cooperating with each other. It has been found that there exists a Nash equilibrium in this Oligopoly market which is a set of outputs, such that each seller's output is the best response to those of the others [15].

The assumptions of our Cournot's Oligopoly model-based scheme are as follows:

- Participant i's output: $q_i = \mathbb{E}[s^{i,d(l,t,AQI)}]$.
- Total output: $q = q_1 + q_2 + \cdots + q_n$, where n is the total number of participants who have the report at location l.
- The opponents' output: $q_{-i} = q - q_i = \sum_{j \neq i} q_j$.
- The constant marginal cost of participant i (location privacy loss): c_i.
- Inverse demand function: $m(q) = A - Bq$.

4.3.2.1   Participants' Upload Strategy

Using the Oligopoly model, the benefit participant i is calculated as

$$u_i(s_i, s_{-i}) = m(q) \times q_i - c_i \times q_i. \tag{4.33}$$

To find the value of q_i which maximizes the profit of participant i given q_{-i}, let

$$\frac{\partial u_i}{\partial q_i} = \frac{\partial m(q)}{\partial q_i} \times q_i + m - c_i. \tag{4.34}$$

From

$$\frac{\partial m(q)}{\partial q_i} \times q_i + m - c_i = 0, \tag{4.35}$$

substituting $m(q) = A - Bq$, we have

$$-Bq_i + A - Bq - c_i = 0. \tag{4.36}$$

This yields the n simultaneous equations:

$$-Bq_1 + A - Bq - c_1 = 0 \tag{4.37}$$
$$-Bq_2 + A - Bq - c_2 = 0 \tag{4.38}$$

$$\vdots$$

$$-Bq_n + A - Bq - c_n = 0. \tag{4.39}$$

The summation of above equations yields

$$-Bq + nA - nBq - n \times \bar{c} = 0, \tag{4.40}$$

where $\bar{c} = \frac{c_1 + c_2 + \cdots + c_n}{n}$. Thus we can deduce the total output q as:

$$q = \frac{n}{n+1} \frac{A - \bar{c}}{B}, \tag{4.41}$$

and each participant's output q_i in the n-Cournot Oligopoly model is

$$q_i = \frac{1}{n+1} \frac{A}{B} + \frac{n(\bar{c} - c_i) - c_i}{(n+1)B}. \tag{4.42}$$

Specifically, if all the participants have identical marginal costs $c_i = \bar{c} = c$, then

$$q_i = \frac{1}{n+1} \frac{A - c}{B}. \tag{4.43}$$

4.3.2.2 SP's Pricing Strategy

Similarly with the case in MMBS, the SP's target is to achieve certain QoS, thus

$$q_i = 1 - \sqrt[n]{1 - Q_{th}}. \tag{4.44}$$

Combining (4.41) with

$$m = (A - Bq) \times q, \tag{4.45}$$

we have

$$A = \frac{(n+1)m}{q} - nc, \tag{4.46}$$

and

$$B = \frac{n}{n+1} \frac{A - c}{q}. \tag{4.47}$$

Again we have the constraint that $A - c > 0$, thus

$$m > cq. \tag{4.48}$$

Comparing Equations (4.29) (4.30) with Eqs. (4.46) (4.47), we can find that even with the same budget costs, the SP should set different inverse demand function parameters A and B, due to the different behaviors of the participants.

The process of COMBS is summarized in Algorithm 2.

Algorithm 2: Cournot's Oligopoly Model-Based Scheme (COMBS).

---

1 **Initialization:** Define the targeted QoS Q_{th}, and the participants' cost c.
2 *SP's Pricing Strategy:*
3 **for** $l \in \mathscr{L}$ **do**
4   Allocate the budget $m = \beta cq$, where $\beta > 1$ is the payment factor;
5   Find the expected number of participants n at location l under the budget m;
6   Calculate $q = n(1 - \sqrt[n]{1 - Q_{th}})$;
7   Defining pricing strategy:

$$m(q) = A - Bq,$$

   where

$$A = \frac{(n+1)m}{q} - nc, \quad B = \frac{n}{n+1}\frac{A-c}{q}.$$

   Broadcast A, B and n to all participants.
8 **end**
9 *Participant i 's upload strategy:*
10 **for** $l \in \mathscr{L}$ **do**
11   Calculate $q_i = \frac{1}{n+1}\frac{A-c}{B}$;
12   Set the upload strategy which satisfies: $Pr\{s^{i,d \langle l,t,AirQuality \rangle} = 1\} = q_i$.
13 **end**

4.3.3 Privacy Analysis of Our Proposed Schemes

Through the above two economic-based schemes, our proposed privacy-preserving MCS framework could work well without the bidding and task assignment processes. Moreover, we can theoretically prove the effectiveness of our proposed framework.

Theorem 4.1 *In the case of a strong adversary who could capture the data traffic in the communication channel and the data in the SP, our proposed MCS framework can guarantee no worse privacy preservation than the traditional framework.*

Proof Assuming that at a certain location l, there are n participants for the current task duration T. Then in the traditional MCS framework, all the participants who have packets of location l first bid for the task. In case that their bidding information is acquired by the adversary, the overall location privacy loss is

$$LPL_{l,n} = \sum_{1 \leq i \leq n} [H_0(i) - H_T(i)]$$

$$= n \log_2 L. \tag{4.49}$$

On the other hand, with our proposed scheme, only the participants who actually upload their packets lose the location privacy at location l, thus

$$LPL_{l,n} = \sum_{1 \leq i \leq n} [H_0(i) - H_T(i)]$$

$$= \sum_{1 \leq i \leq n} s^{i,d\langle l,t,AirQuality\rangle} \log_2 L \qquad \leq n \log_2 L. \tag{4.50}$$

As in both MMBS- and COMBS-based schemes, we have

$$\mathbb{E}\left[\sum_{p \in \mathscr{P}, t \in \mathscr{T}} s^{p,d\langle l,t,AQI\rangle}\right] = \mathbb{E}\left[\sum_{1 \leq i \leq n} s^{i,d\langle l,t,AirQuality\rangle}\right] = q, \tag{4.51}$$

therefore

$$\mathbb{E}[LPL_{l,n}] = q \log_2 L$$

$$= n(1 - \sqrt[n]{1 - Q_{th}}) \log_2 L$$

$$\leq n \log_2 L. \tag{4.52}$$

where the equal sign applies if and only if $Q_{th} = 1$, which is not necessary in most applications.

Figures 4.2 and 4.3 give some example results of the above proof. It can be seen that the proposed framework can greatly reduce the number of upload packets so as to

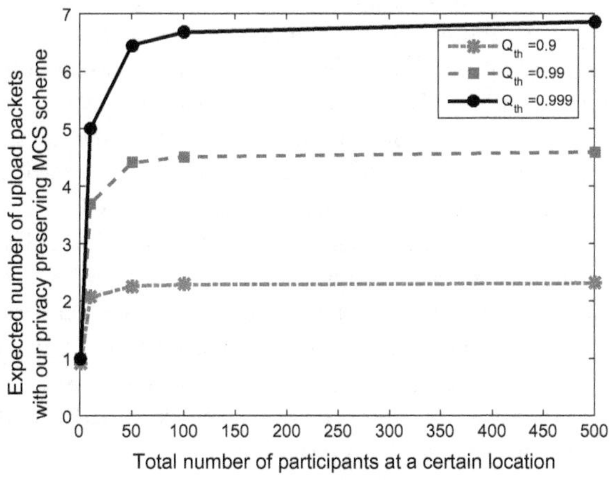

Fig. 4.2 The theoretical upload packet number with our privacy-preserving MCS framework

Fig. 4.3 Comparison of
location privacy loss
between the traditional and
our privacy-preserving MCS
frameworks (L = 25)

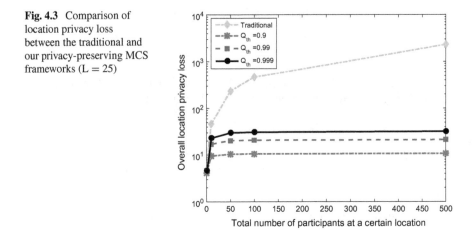

reduce the LPL for most of the scenarios ($Q_{th} < 1$). For example, when $Q_{th} = 0.99$,
when the total number of participants is 100, only about 4.5 among them need to
upload packets under of privacy-preserving MCS framework (as shown in Fig. 4.2).
And the LPL will be reduced from around 5000 to only about 20, as shown in Fig. 4.3.

4.4 Performance Evaluation

4.4.1 Simulation Setup

The empirical evaluation is performed using the GPS trajectory dataset Geolife collected by Microsoft Research Asia which contains 17,621 trajectories of 182 users
in Beijing area in a period of over three years [16–18]. These trajectories recorded a
broad range of users' outdoor movements, including not only life routines but also
some entertainments and sports activities, such as shopping, sightseeing, dining, hik-
ing, and cycling. It has been used in many research fields, such as mobility pattern
mining, user activity recognition, location-based social networks, location privacy,
and location recommendation. However, as the dataset is not collected specifically
for the purpose of MCS applications, some preprocessing works need to be done
before it can be used for simulation.

First, we select the data between November 1, 2008 and November 7, 2008 which
include a comparably high volume of location information. Then in the spatial dimen-
sion, a 20 km × 30 km area is divided into 5 × 5 4 km × 6 km small cells (discrete
locations). The described area and participants' trajectories in this area are shown in
Fig. 4.4. If a certain participant p's trajectory passes a cell l, it means $l \in \mathcal{L}_{p,T}$.

Moreover, the raw trajectories were recorded with high sampling rates, i.e., every
1~5 s or every 5~10 m per point. We downsample the raw data, keeping only one

Fig. 4.4 Map of the area for simulation (green lines indicate the participants' trajectories)

point left in each cell for every participant, to obtain a set which consists of 312 trajectories (each trajectory belongs to one participant). And the length of location information set equals to the number of cells they cover. The number of points in each cell and the distribution of lengths of location information set are shown in Figs. 4.5 and 4.6, respectively.

4.4.2 Performance Analysis

We now evaluate the performance of our schemes through extensive simulations. All the results are averaged over 1000 simulations.

4.4.2.1 Performance of MMBS

First we consider the SP's cost. The SP first decides the expected number of upload data packets in each cell, according to the targeted QoS. For example, when $Q_{th} =$

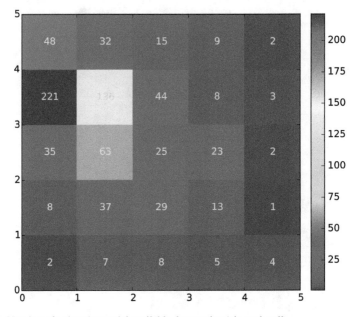

Fig. 4.5 Number of points (potential available data packets) in each cell

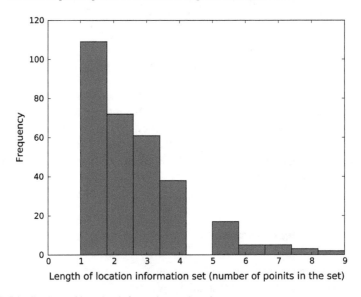

Fig. 4.6 Distributions of location information set lengths

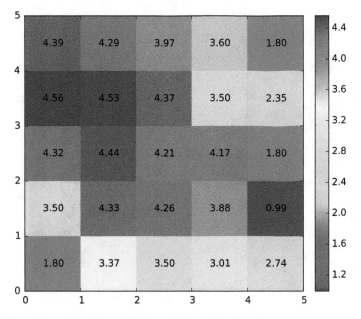

Fig. 4.7 Expected number of upload data packets in each cell

0.99, the expected q can be obtained using Eq. (4.27), and the results are illustrated in Fig. 4.7. Furthermore, according to the constraint of budget, we can obtain the SP's budget for each cell. Figure 4.8 shows the budget when $m = 2cq$ and $c = \alpha \cdot LPL_{p,l} = \log_2 L = 4.6439$ where $\alpha = 1$ and $L = 25$.

From the analysis in Sect. 4.3, we can see that the SP's budget is decided by the privacy cost c and the targeted QoS. Figure 4.10 illustrates the relationship between the targeted QoS and the SP's budget. We see a dramatic budget increase as the QoS grows from 0.99 to 0.999 which means the price to gain slight rise in QoS above 99% is quite high. Moreover, the SP's actual cost which is obtained by simulation is a slightly lower than the budget, due to the approximation between expectation value and actual upload number following the probability. To be more specific, the theoretical cost is

$$m = (A - Bq) \times q$$

$$= A \cdot \mathbb{E}\left[\sum_{p \in \mathcal{P}, t \in \mathcal{T}} s^{p,d\langle l,t,AQI\rangle}\right]$$

$$- B \cdot \left(\mathbb{E}\left[\sum_{p \in \mathcal{P}, t \in \mathcal{T}} s^{p,d\langle l,t,AQI\rangle}\right]\right)^2, \tag{4.53}$$

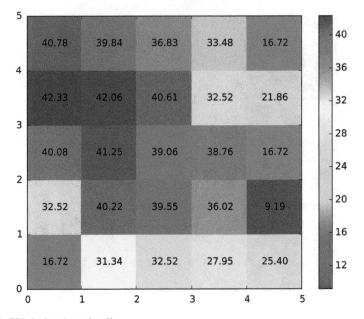

Fig. 4.8 SP's budget in each cell

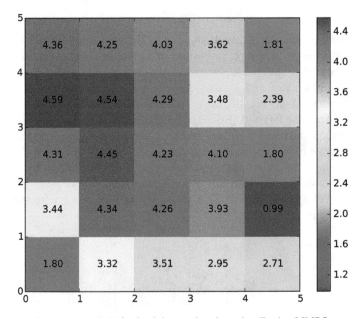

Fig. 4.9 Actual average number of upload data packets in each cell using MMBS

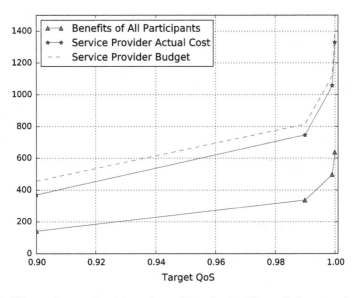

Fig. 4.10 SP's actual cost and participants' overall benefit with different QoS targets using MMBS

while the actual cost is

$$\mathbb{E}\left[A \cdot \sum_{p\in\mathcal{P},t\in\mathcal{T}} s^{p,d\langle l,t,AQI\rangle}\right]$$
$$-\mathbb{E}\left[B \cdot \left(\sum_{p\in\mathcal{P},t\in\mathcal{T}} s^{p,d\langle l,t,AQI\rangle}\right)^2\right]. \tag{4.54}$$

As

$$B \cdot \left(\mathbb{E}\left[\sum_{p\in\mathcal{P},t\in\mathcal{T}} s^{p,d\langle l,t,AQI\rangle}\right]\right)^2$$
$$\leq \mathbb{E}\left[B \cdot \left(\sum_{p\in\mathcal{P},t\in\mathcal{T}} s^{p,d\langle l,t,AQI\rangle}\right)^2\right], \tag{4.55}$$

the actual payments from the SP to the participants are lower than the theoretical value.

And the actual upload packets' number in each cell is also slightly different from the expected value for the same reason, as shown in Fig. 4.9.

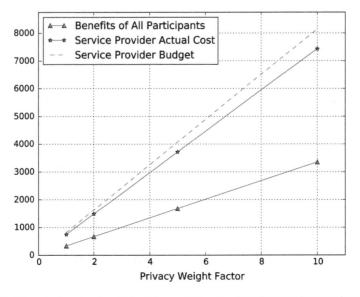

Fig. 4.11 SP's actual cost and participants' overall benefit with different privacy weight factor α using MMBS

With regard to the privacy cost, Fig. 4.11 shows the linear relationship between the SP's budget and participants' privacy weight factor α, which means the SP has to provide more incentives when the participants emphasize more on their privacy.

On the other hand, when the SP decides its budgets according to the Monopoly model, the participants' overall benefit peaks at the best upload probability (calculated with Eq. (4.22)), as shown in Fig. 4.12. Moreover, the achieved QoS with the best upload probability satisfies the SP's expectation at the same time. It is important to note that the best upload probability varies with the number of available data packets in each cell. For example, the best upload probability of cell (4, 2) which we use to plot Fig. 4.12 is 0.26. Simulations show that the participants' overall benefits always peak at the best upload probabilities for all cells.

Focusing on the location privacy degree loss, Fig. 4.13 compares the histograms of location privacy degrees before and after the MCS task. It can be seen that the number of participants with high location privacy degrees (bigger than 20) declines after the task, which means that the uploaded data packets are prone to come from the long location information sets. This is beneficial for participants who have lower location privacy degrees to avoid being fully exposed. On the other hand, the average location privacy degree loss is less than 10% in most cases, as shown in Fig. 4.14, which makes our scheme quite attractive from the perspective of privacy preservation.

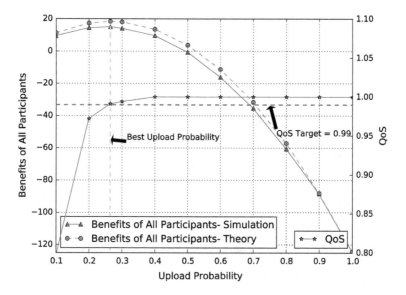

Fig. 4.12 Participants' overall benefits with different upload probabilities in cell (4, 2) using MMBS

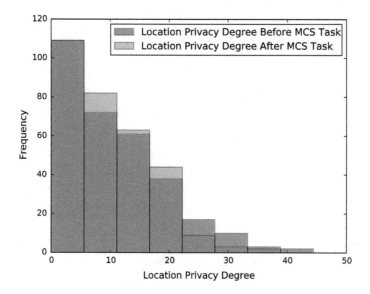

Fig. 4.13 Distribution of participants' privacy degrees before and after the MCS task using MMBS

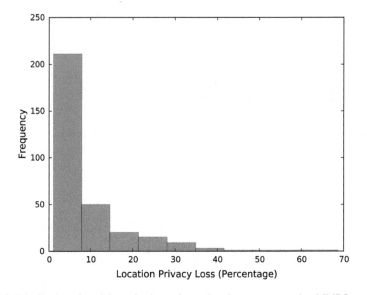

Fig. 4.14 Distribution of participants' privacy degree loss in percentage using MMBS

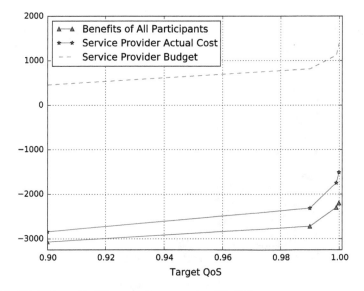

Fig. 4.15 SP's budget with different QoS targets using COMBS

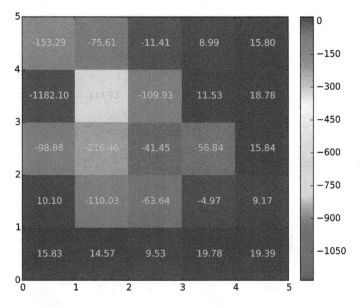

Fig. 4.16 SP's actual cost in different cells using COMBS

4.4.2.2 Performance of COMBS

When evaluating the performance of COMBS, we the use same budget amount $m = 2cq$. But the values of parameters A and B are different, due to the distinctions between Eqs. (4.29) (4.30) and Eqs. (4.46) (4.47). We plot the SP's budget, SP's actual cost, and participants' benefits in Fig. 4.15. The figure shows a big gap between the SP's budget and actual cost, which is caused by the approximation from the expectation to the actual value, as explained by Eqs. (4.53)–(4.55). The gap is much bigger than the case in MMBS, because the values of A and B in inverse demand function of COMBS are bigger than those of MMBS (compare equations (4.29) (4.30) and (4.46) (4.47)).

In order to better understand the reason for this phenomenon, we compute the SP's average cost in each cell, as shown in Fig. 4.16. Comparing Fig. 4.16 with Figs. 4.8 and 4.5, it can be concluded that although using the same SP budget as that in MMBS, the actual cost of COMBS is biased away from expectation. Moreover, the bias is enlarged when the number of available points is big. For instance, the actual cost of cell $(0, 3)$ (221 points) is only about -1182, while the cost of cell $(4, 1)$ (only 1 point) is exactly the same as the budget.

Now, we evaluate the performance of COMBS from the participants' perspective. Theoretically, a certain participant's benefit should be maximized with the best Oligopoly upload probability, which means he can gain no more profit while all others use the best Oligopoly upload probabilities. However, the actual upload number for a certain participant is either 1 or 0, instead of the expectation value q_i,

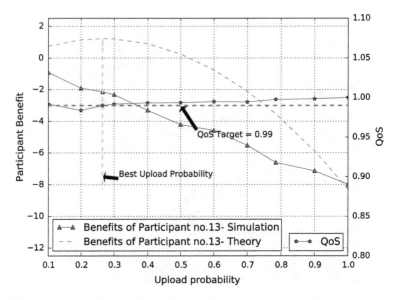

Fig. 4.17 One participant's (no. 13) benefit with different upload probabilities in cell (4, 2) using COMBS.eps

which makes the actual cases different. Figures 4.17 and 4.18 give two examples of the actual benefit. The participant no. 13 can obtain more benefit when he chooses smaller upload probability, while the participant no. 117 gains more when selecting bigger probability. In fact, we find that when the theoretical best Oligopoly upload probability in a given cell is smaller than 0.5, the corresponding participant's benefit curve will be a descending one similar to the case in Fig. 4.17. On the contrary, the curve is ascending when the theoretical probability is bigger than 0.5.

Finally, from the perspective of location privacy degree loss, COMBS achieves similar privacy degree preservation with that of MMBS, as shown in Figs. 4.19 and 4.20.

4.4.3   Discussions

Overall, due to the deviation between the expectation number (which equals the probability) and actual number (either 1 or 0) of upload packets from each participant, the performances of both MMBS and COMBS witness margins to analytical values. Specifically, from the perspective of participants' overall benefits, the performance of MMBS is still close to the theoretical threshold as the model targets on finding the best total upload packets of all participants, while the COMBS experiences more bias when it tries to find the optimal upload strategy for each participant. These results demonstrate that the MMBS is more suitable for the studied air pollution monitoring

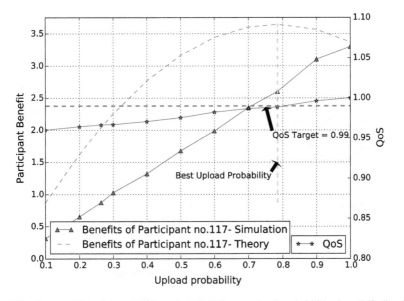

Fig. 4.18 One participant's (no. 117) benefit with different upload probabilities in cell (3, 4) using COMBS

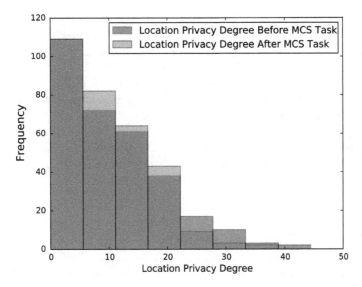

Fig. 4.19 Distribution of participants' location privacy degrees before and after the MCS task using COMBS

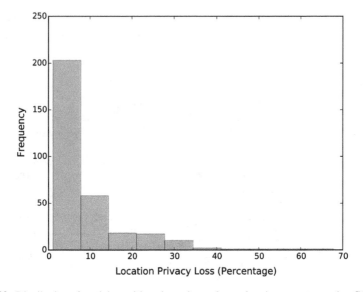

Fig. 4.20 Distribution of participants' location privacy degree loss in percentage using COMBS

application in this chapter, in which we assume that only one packet at a certain location l is needed during one sensing task duration. In other applications which need more outputs for a certain type, the COMBS should have better performance. To support the statement, we rerun the simulation of Fig. 4.17, but treat the q_i in Algorithm 2 as a quantity instead of probability, i.e., if q_i is 0.2643, the participant will upload 0.2643 packets. The result in Fig. 4.21 shows that the benefit of the participant indeed peaks at the best upload quantity.

Finally, we want to further talk about the several parameters in our scheme. In the simulation, we use the real dataset to get the number of participants n at certain location l. In practical MCS applications, n is related to the payment factor β and the relationship could be obtained via analyzing the historical data.

4.5 Conclusions and Future Works

In this chapter, we have studied the location privacy issue of MCS applications. The framework which enhances the location privacy of MCS participants is proposed, by eliminating the general bidding and task assignment processes. Our contributions are threefold. First, the relationship between the SP and participants is modeled as a consumer–producer pair. In addition, two privacy-preserved schemes are designed based on the Monopoly and Oligopoly models, respectively. Based on these schemes, we identify important parameters which affect the SP's cost, targeted QoS and the

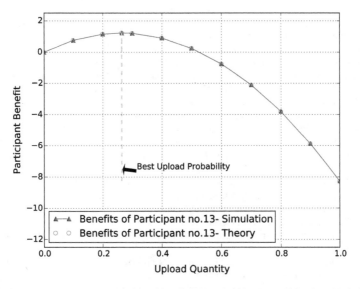

Fig. 4.21 One participant's (no. 13) benefit with different upload quantities in cell (4, 2) using COMBS

participants' utilities. Detailed simulation results and performance analysis validate the effectiveness of the proposed schemes.

There are several interesting directions for future works. First, we can define different QoS requirements for MCS applications. For example, if the SP needs more than one data packets at a certain location at a given time, then the Oligopoly model-based scheme may show better performance. Second, factors such as inverse demand function can be changed to fit different cases. Finally, it is also interesting to further investigate corresponding schemes when the privacy degree for each point is weighted differently.

References

1. B. Liu, W. Zhou, T. Zhu, H. Zhou, X. Lin, Invisible hand: a privacy preserving mobile crowd sensing framework based on economic models. IEEE Trans. Veh. Technol. **66**(5), 4410–4423 (2017)
2. B. Guo, Z. Yu, X. Zhou, D. Zhang, From participatory sensing to mobile crowd sensing, in *Proceedings of the IEEE PERCOM Workshops* (2014), pp. 593–598
3. R.K. Ganti, F. Ye, H. Lei, Mobile crowdsensing: current state and future challenges. IEEE Commun. Mag. **49**(11), 32–39 (2011)
4. P. Dutta, P.M. Aoki, N. Kumar, A. Mainwaring, C. Myers, W. Willett, A. Woodruff, Common sense: participatory urban sensing using a network of handheld air quality monitors, in *Proceedings of the 7th ACM Conference on Embedded Networked Sensor Systems*, ACM (2009), pp. 349–350

5. V. Sivaraman, J. Carrapetta, K. Hu, B.G. Luxan, Hazewatch: a participatory sensor system for monitoring air pollution in sydney, in *IEEE 38th Conference on Local Computer Networks Workshops (LCN Workshops)*, IEEE (2013), pp. 56–64

6. R.K. Rana, C.T. Chou, S.S. Kanhere, N. Bulusu, W. Hu, Ear-phone: an end-to-end participatory urban noise mapping system, in *Proceedings of the 9th ACM/IEEE International Conference on Information Processing in Sensor Networks*, ACM (2010), pp. 105–116

7. B. Hull, V. Bychkovsky, Y. Zhang, K. Chen, M. Goraczko, A. Miu, E. Shih, H. Balakrishnan, S. Madden, Cartel: a distributed mobile sensor computing system, in *Proceedings of the 4th International Conference on Embedded Networked Sensor Systems*, ACM (2006), pp. 125–138

8. P. Mohan, V.N. Padmanabhan, R. Ramjee, Nericell: rich monitoring of road and traffic conditions using mobile smartphones, in *Proceedings of the 6th ACM Conference on Embedded Network Sensor Systems*, ACM (2008), pp. 323–336

9. S. Reddy, A. Parker, J. Hyman, J. Burke, D. Estrin, M. Hansen, Image browsing, processing, and clustering for participatory sensing: lessons from a dietsense prototype, in *Proceedings of the 4th Workshop on Embedded Networked Sensors*, ACM (2007), pp. 13–17

10. S.B. Eisenman, E. Miluzzo, N.D. Lane, R.A. Peterson, G.-S. Ahn, A.T. Campbell, Bikenet: a mobile sensing system for cyclist experience mapping. ACM Trans. Sens. Netw. (TOSN) **6**(1), 6 (2009)

11. L. Kong, L. He, X.-Y. Liu, Y. Gu, M.-Y. Wu, X. Liu, Privacy-preserving compressive sensing for crowdsensing based trajectory recovery

12. D. Zhao, X.-Y. Li, H. Ma, How to crowdsource tasks truthfully without sacrificing utility: online incentive mechanisms with budget constraint, in *Proceedings of the IEEE INFOCOM* (2014), pp. 1213–1221

13. A. Serjantov, G. Danezis, Towards an Information Theoretic Metric for Anonymity, in *Proceeding of 2nd International Conference on Privacy Enhancing Technology* (2003), pp. 41–53

14. B. Hoh, M. Gruteser, Protecting location privacy through path confusion, in *Proceedings of the IEEE SecureComm* (2005), pp. 194–205

15. C.A. Holt, *Markets, Games, and Strategic Behavior: Recipes for Interactive Learning* (Addison Wesley, Reading, 2006)

16. Y. Zheng, L. Zhang, X. Xie, W.-Y. Ma, Mining interesting locations and travel sequences from GPS trajectories, in *Proceedings of the ACM International Conference on World Wide Web* (2009), pp. 791–800

17. Y. Zheng, Q. Li, Y. Chen, X. Xie, W.-Y. Ma, Understanding mobility based on GPS data, in *Proceedings of the ACM International Conference on Ubiquitous Computing* (2008), pp. 312–321

18. Y. Zheng, X. Xie, W.-Y. Ma, Geolife: a collaborative social networking service among user, location and trajectory. IEEE Data Eng. Bull. **33**(2), 32–39 (2010)

Chapter 5
Location Privacy in Wireless Vehicular Networks

In the scenario of vehicular networks, due to connectivity transitory and throughput degradation caused by high vehicle mobility, traditional privacy-preserving methods such as k-anonymity are not sufficient. As an effort toward this issue, we propose a framework which enhances the privacy of LBS by actively caching in the wireless vehicular network scenario [1]. The scheme is designed under the dedicated short-range communication (DSRC) standard, with three original contributions. First, a point of interest (POI) query probability model for in-vehicle users is defined, considering the spatial relationship between the current location and the queried location. Second, three broadcasting content selection algorithms of the roadside unit (RSU) are proposed, including two adaptive updating methods and one knowledge-based pre-caching method. Third, we identify critical parameters that affect the privacy, including RSU distance, vehicle speed, query set size of POI, size of each POI entry, and the proportion of channel capacity used for RSU broadcast (defined as channel occupancy). Lastly, the proposed scheme is evaluated by extensive simulations and the results are discussed in detail.

The reminder of the chapter is organized as follows. Section 5.1 briefly introduces the research background. Section 5.2 describes preliminary models. The problem formulation and the details of our proposed scheme are presented in Sect. 5.3. Section 5.4 gives the performance simulation results and analysis, as well as the comparison with other methods. Finally, Sect. 5.5 draws the conclusion about this paper.

5.1 Introduction

Most of the existing privacy protection methods are mainly designed for static environment with low mobility of users. The LBS applications of fast-motion users, such as in vehicles, are however rarely studied before. Notably, in-vehicle users might query for the available gas stations or restaurants within the next 50 km, or they might need to periodically retrieve the traffic information. In these occasions,

© The Author(s), under exclusive licence to Springer Nature Singapore Pte Ltd. 2018
B. Liu et al., *Location Privacy in Mobile Applications*,
SpringerBriefs on Cyber Security Systems and Networks,
https://doi.org/10.1007/978-981-13-1705-7_5

traditional privacy protection methods might not be sufficient due to the unique challenges brought by the highly dynamic vehicular network environment from the following two aspects. First, the wireless connectivity from vehicles to communication infrastructures, such as base stations, and between vehicles are both transitory due to the high vehicle mobility. This increases the difficulty of identifying a proper community for anonymization-based methods. Second, the throughput performance of the cellular network degrades significantly due to severe Doppler shift and multipath fading in the highly mobile environment. This will further increase the cost of obtaining data. In this case, caching the service data obtained for the dummy locations of the queries as in [2] might not be effective any more. Finally, as there typically exist a large number of vehicles contending the channel for transmissions in vehicular networks, increasing query numbers to achieve k-anonymity will aggravate the channel contention problem.

It is, however, important to note that the unique features of vehicular networks as well as the in-vehicle users can be leveraged to improve the privacy preservation. First, the dedicated short-range communication (DSRC) technology has been developed to support vehicle-to-vehicle (V2V) and vehicle-to-roadside (V2R) communications, using the exclusive 75 MHz of licensed spectrum in the 5.9 GHz band [3]. Under this framework, vehicles are possible to acquire temporary and opportunistic wireless connections to the Internet when driving through the coverage of wireless roadside gateway points, namely roadside units (RSUs). This network infrastructure, therefore, might be used to provide LBSs with low cost and high throughput. Meanwhile, the queries from in-vehicle users are highly coherent in space and time, as their trajectories and destinations have predictable trends. For example, a user at home may query a POI which is thousands of miles away as he plans to travel at vocations. However, an in-vehicle user is more likely to query for a nearby location which he can arrive at within one hour. Such feature can help select some highly probably queried data for in-vehicle users.

As motivated by the observations above, in this chapter, we develop an LBS privacy-enhancing scheme which is dedicated to the vehicular environment by exploring the unique features of queries from in-vehicle users. The proposed tripartite coordination mechanism involves the RSU, the on-board unit (OBU) operated on DSRC band, and the in-vehicle user. The basic idea of our proposal is by utilizing OBUs to actively download and cache the data periodically broadcasted by RSUs. When an in-vehicle user requests for the POI information, he first checks with the OBU to avoid issuing duplicate or highly coherent queries to the LBS server, either via the RSU or other channels such as the cellular network. We assume that the OBU is trustworthy, as it is installed on the user's own vehicle. The RSU, however, might not be trustworthy, and therefore, the interactions between the RSU and the user should be reduced as many as possible. This target is achieved by RSU content broadcasting and OBU active caching. Additionally, we propose a POI query probability model based on the space correlation property. Then, the content of RSU broadcasting is selected accordingly to enhance the user's privacy, either by adaptive updating algorithms or knowledge-based pre-caching method.

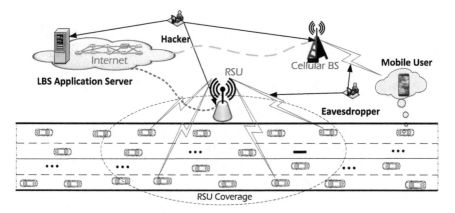

Fig. 5.1 Scenario of the wireless vehicular network on the highway

5.2 System Model

5.2.1 *System Model*

We consider the highway wireless vehicular network scenario, as shown in Fig. 5.1. RSUs from a set $\mathscr{R}$ are installed on the roadside with a given distance d_{rsu} between two consecutive ones, which serve as the gateways to provide network services to vehicles (from a set $\mathscr{V}$) driving through their coverage areas. Meanwhile, the cellular network coexists with the vehicular network, and the vehicles are equipped with OBUs. The mobile clients (i.e., mobile devices such as smartphones, tablets) used by passengers in the vehicles have cellular interfaces which are used to communicate with cellular base stations (BSs), and Wi-Fi interfaces which enable data exchange with the OBUs. As the gateways between clients and RSUs, the OBUs support DSRC interfaces. The RSUs are linked with the servers located in the Internet through high-speed backhaul links for data upload and download.

When users in a certain area send LBS queries (from the set $\mathscr{Q}$) to obtain information of some POIs from the set $\mathscr{P}$, either the OBUs or LBS servers will respond by sending packs of information contents which belong to the set $\mathscr{C}$. Although there might be multiple users in one vehicle, their privacy issues can be equally treated. Therefore, the set of users are also represented by the set of vehicles in our paper. Moreover, for $\mathscr{R}, \mathscr{V}, \mathscr{Q}, \mathscr{P}, \mathscr{C}$, their sizes and general representations of elements are R, V, Q, P, C and r, v, q, p, c, respectively. Important symbols used in this paper are listed in Table 5.1 for reference.

Table 5.1 Summary of important symbols

$\mathcal{R}, \mathcal{V}, \mathcal{P}, \mathcal{C}, \mathcal{Q}$	The RSU, vehicle, the POI, the information content, and the LBS query sets
R, V, P, C, Q	The sizes of the RSU, vehicle, the POI, the information content, and the LBS query sets
r, v, p, c, q	The elements of the RSU, vehicle, the POI, the information content, and the LBS query sets
$v_i(t)$	The velocity of vehicle i at time t
Γ	A vehicle's sojourn time within RSU's coverage
d_{rsu}	The distance between two consecutive RSUs
ζ	The RSU coverage range (communication zone)
η	The application layer data rate of the RSU broadcasting
η_{max}	The maximum application layer data rate of the RSU broadcasting
η_{PHY}	The maximum physical layer data rate of the RSU broadcasting
T_S	The sync period of DSRC, including one CCH interval and one SCH interval
T_{GI}	The guard interval period of DSRC
T_{CCH}	The duration of one CCH interval of DSRC
T_{SCH}	The duration of one SCH interval of DSRC
T_{LBS}	The duration of LBS information broadcast in one SCH interval
λ_I	The individual average privacy degree
λ_G	The global privacy degree

5.2.2 V2R Communication Model

Our scheme is designed under the DSRC standard which has been developed for wireless vehicular communication, including both V2V and V2R communications.

At the physical (PHY) layer and MAC layer, DSRC utilizes IEEE 802.11p Wireless Access for Vehicular Environments (WAVE) [4], which is a modified version of the familiar IEEE 802.11 (Wi-Fi) standard. The bandwidth of WAVE is $10MHz$. Moreover, 802.11p design has proven very efficient in reducing MAC layer overhead with respect to the legacy 802.11 protocol, with the application layer throughput achieving about 83% of the PHY raw data rate [5].

In the proposed scheme, we use the lowest data rate and largest communication zone to ensure the highest efficiency of content dissemination. As the PHY data rate η_{PHY} is 3 Mbps, the highest achievable application layer data rate η_{max} is around 2 Mbps. The parameters used for V2R communications are summarized in Table 5.2.

DSRC employs a data structure as shown in Fig. 5.2 [6]. It is constructed based on the time division concept. The control channel (CCH) is a special rendezvous channel that the devices will tune to on a regular basis. All other channels in the band plan are designated as service channels (SCH). During a CCH interval devices wishing to find each other rendezvous on the CCH where they may hear WAVE

Table 5.2 Parameters used for V2R communications

Parameter	Value
Bandwidth	10 MHz
PHY layer data rate η_{PHY}	3 Mbps (BPSK, 1/2 coding rate)
Maximum app layer data rate η_{max}	2 Mbps
RSU communication zone ζ	1000 m (Class D device)

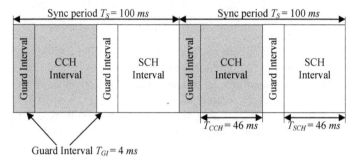

Fig. 5.2 Division of time into CCH intervals and SCH intervals in DSRC

Service Advertisement (WSA) announcing the availability of any services offered in the immediate area. The WSA provides information about one or more services and indicates the SCH on which each service is offered. During an SCH interval, devices may switch to one of the SCHs. Therefore, the SCH intervals can be used to deliver data such as the LBS-related information [7].

Assuming that the LBS data are uniformly delivered among the sync period and T_{LBS} is used for this service in each SCH internal, then the application layer data rate of the LBS data delivery is:

$$\eta = \eta_{max} \frac{T_{LBS}}{T_S}. \tag{5.1}$$

Also, we define the channel occupancy (ChO) as

Definition 5.1 (*Channel occupancy*) The percentage of the LBS delivery data rate within the total available data rate.

And we have

$$ChO = \frac{T_{LBS}}{T_S} = \frac{\eta}{\eta_{max}}. \tag{5.2}$$

5.2.3   Privacy Threats for In-Vehicle Users and Adversary Attack Models

We now discuss the privacy threats for in-vehicle users when using LBSs. Whenever a user starts an LBS, he first needs to submit queries which include his location information, through a particular LBS application such as TripAdvisor. According to the different conditions that the LBS query is sent once or multiple times, the services provided are named *snapshot* LBS and *continuous* LBS, respectively. Then, if the adversary obtains the LBS information, the *point location privacy* and *trajectory privacy* are leaked accordingly.

In-vehicle users may face both two types of privacy challenges. For example, the local POI search (e.g., searching restaurants within a user-specified range distance) has the risk of point location privacy leakage, while the navigation service exposes the locations on the trajectory continuously.

With regard to the adversary model, we consider two possible types of adversary attacks in the above-described LBS process in vehicular networks (also illustrated in Fig. 5.1).

5.2.3.1   Eavesdropper Attack

An eavesdropper could capture the data traffic between RSUs and OBUs, in-vehicle users and cellular BSs, via monitoring the wireless channels.

5.2.3.2   Hacker Attack

Due to the fact that there exist a large number of RSUs, cost considerations prevent the RSUs from having sufficient protection from hacker attacks. Moreover, the LBS servers or cellular BSs might be hijacked as well. Therefore, a hacker might access and obtain all data in some RSUs, cellular BSs, or the LBS servers.

On the other hand, the OBU and its link with the in-vehicle user are assumed to be secure. First, the OBU is equipped in the vehicle and its mobility greatly reduces the attack chances from the adversary. Moreover, as the link between the OBU and the user is restricted within a small range in the cabin, it is also difficult for the eavesdropper attack to take place.

5.2.4   POI Query Probability

Assume that an in-vehicle user sends a query q, the current location of the vehicle is l_v and the query location is l_q (i.e., the user wants to obtain POI information near l_q). Since users traveling on the highway are more likely to query for POIs nearby, the probability of querying location l_q decreases with its Euclid distance to l_v. In a continuous case, the Gaussian distribution can be used to present this property. However, here we have a discrete case in which one probability should be assigned to each possible distance value and the summation of probabilities at all locations should equal to 1. Therefore, we define the probability mass function for querying location l_q when the location of the vehicle is l_v as

$$Prob(l_q, l_v) = \frac{e^{-Euc(l_q,l_v)}}{\sum\limits_{q \in \mathcal{Q}^v} e^{-Euc(l_q,l_v)}}, \tag{5.3}$$

and

$$\sum\limits_{q \in \mathcal{Q}^v} Prob(l_q, l_v) = 1. \tag{5.4}$$

5.3 Problem Formulation and the Proposed Privacy-Enhancing Scheme

5.3.1 Basic Idea of Our Privacy Preservation Framework

Based on the adversary attack models, only the OBU and its link with the in-vehicle user are secure. Therefore, in order to improve the privacy degree, we need to reduce the number of queries which are not answered by the OBUs. A straightforward idea is to use the cache method. But common cache methods may not work well in our scenario. For example, one could pre-download maps and POIs in some applications such as HERE Drive+. However, this model does not work well for contents which change frequently such as social events, special daily offer of restaurant, movie schedulers, and flyers. Moreover, as users' requests are both limited and time variant, pre-downloading maps of all areas is often a waste of the storage resource.

To address the aforementioned problem, our motivation is trying to reduce the number of queries while not affecting the freshness of the content. First, let us revisit the background of vehicular network. If a vehicle is equipped with an OBU and it is within the coverage area of an RSU, this service can be completed through the RSU, besides the traditional method of mobile user submitting it directly via the cellular base station. However, the privacy of the in-vehicle user is in danger since the submitted query includes the user's location, no matter which channel is used. On the contrary, if a user could obtain the LBS information without sending queries, the privacy will be preserved. Therefore, we can use the RSU to broadcast POI data. As the broadcasting is an one-way communication channel, the information contained in the broadcasting content does not leak any privacy related to any specific user. We require no intercommunication between the RSU and the OBU. The OBU keeps silent to prevent the privacy leakage.

Fig. 5.3 Data flow of our proposed scheme: (1) The mobile user first sends the query to the OBU; (2.1) if the required data are not in the OBU cache and the vehicle is in the coverage area of RSU, (3.1) the query is sent via OBU and RSU; (2.2) if the required data are not in the OBU cache and the vehicle is not in the coverage area of RSU, (3.2) the query is sent through the cellular network

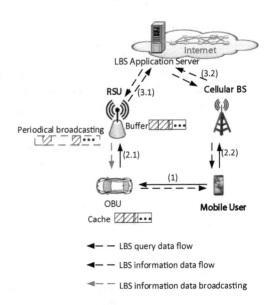

Based on the above analysis, we have the idea of broadcasting and *active caching*, i.e., pushing some popular contents via the RSU and cache them in the OBU. It is called *active caching* because the OBU could actively receive and cache the LBS information from the broadcasting content before the in-vehicle user has issued the related queries, while in common cache methods only the contents related to previous queries are stored. Therefore, with the proposed framework, the in-vehicle users could obtain the LBS information directly from the OBUs in the future.

Figure 5.3 further illustrates our basic idea, which can be explained from viewpoints of the user and the RSU, respectively. For an in-vehicle user, when he initiates an LBS query, the cache of the trusted OBU will be checked first; if the OBU has the required information, it will reply to the user directly. Otherwise, this OBU checks whether it is in the coverage area of the RSU. If the answer is yes, it will send the query via the RSU; otherwise, the cellular network has to be involved. As for the RSU, it broadcasts the contents in its buffer with an arbitrary data rate η. If there are some queries for new data, it forwards the query to the LBS server, obtains the data, sends to the user, and keeps the data in the buffer for future broadcasting.

5.3.2   Location Privacy Metrics

Before mathematically formulating our problem, we have to define the privacy metrics. There are many metrics to measure the privacy, such as entropy-based metrics [8] and distortion-based metrics [9]. Entropy can be seen as the uncertainty in determining the real location of a user from all the candidates, and it has been widely used in the literature. However, with our adversary attack models and our framework discussed in the above subsection, the privacy of a certain user is either completely protected (the query is answered by the OBU) or leaked (the query is not answered by the OBU). Assuming a user v sends one LBS query q and the location information preservation probability of this query is $\tau^{v,q}$, then

$$\tau^{v,q} = \begin{cases} 0, & (not\ answered\ by\ the\ OBU) \\ 1, & (answered\ by\ the\ OBU) \end{cases} \tag{5.5}$$

Therefore, instead of using entropy, we define a new privacy metric named privacy degree.

Definition 5.2 (*Privacy degree*) The percentage of queries responded by the OBU.

(1) Individual average privacy degree: If a user sends Q^v queries in total, then the probability of location information preservation is

$$\lambda_I = \frac{\sum\limits_{q \in \mathcal{Q}^v} \tau^{v,q}}{Q^v}. \tag{5.6}$$

(2) Global privacy degree: The privacy metric defined in Eq. (5.6) describes the privacy degree achieved for a single user. For all users in the system, the overall privacy degree can be calculated by another metric

$$\lambda_G = \frac{\sum\limits_{v \in \mathcal{V}, q \in \mathcal{Q}} \tau^{v,q}}{Q}. \tag{5.7}$$

Moreover, as the individual privacy degree might be random if the number of queries is small, we will focus on the global privacy degree in the rest part of this paper.

5.3.3 Problem Formulation

Now, we can formulate the problem under our privacy preservation framework.

At a given time t, for each $v \in \mathcal{V}$, its information content in the OBU cache is represented by an R-dimensional vector $c_t^v = (c_t^{v,1}, c_t^{v,2}, ..., c_t^{v,R})$, where $c_t^{v,r}, r \in \mathcal{R}$ denotes the content received by v and from RSU r until time t and the size of content satisfies $C_t^{v,r} = \eta^r \Gamma^{v,r}$. η^r is the broadcasting data rate of RSU r, and $\Gamma^{v,r}$ is v's sojourn time within r's communication zone (calculated using the vehicular mobility model in Appendix A).

Moreover, at a given time t, for each $r \in \mathcal{R}$, its information content in the buffer is represented by a P-dimensional vector $c_t^r = (I_t^{r,1}c^1, I_t^{r,2}c^2, ..., I_t^{r,P}c^P)$, where $I_t^{r,p} =$

$1, p \in \mathscr{P}$ denotes the information c^p of the POI p is currently in the broadcasting buffer of RSU r.

Based on the above notations and assumptions, the privacy preservation problem is formulated as a constrained optimization problem and formally given as:

Problem 5.1 (*Privacy Preservation*)

$$\max \ \lambda_G = \frac{\sum\limits_{v \in \mathscr{V}, t \in \mathscr{T}, q \in \mathscr{Q}} \tau_t^{v,q}}{Q}$$

$$s.t. \ c_t^{v,r} \subseteq \sum c_t^r , \ \forall r \in \mathscr{R}, \forall v \in \mathscr{V} \tag{5.8}$$

$$C_t^r \le C_{t,max}^r = \eta^r \Gamma_{max}^{v,r} , \ \forall r \in \mathscr{R}, \forall v \in \mathscr{V} \tag{5.9}$$

$$C_t^{v,r} = \eta^r \Gamma^{v,r} , \ \forall r \in \mathscr{R}, \forall v \in \mathscr{V} \tag{5.10}$$

$$\eta^r \le \eta_{max} \frac{T_{LBS}}{T_S}, \ \forall r \in \mathscr{R} \tag{5.11}$$

where

$$\tau_t^{v,q} = \begin{cases} 1, & (c_t^{v,q} \subseteq c_t^v) \\ 0, & (c_t^{v,q} \nsubseteq c_t^v) \end{cases} \tag{5.12}$$

where $c_t^{v,q}$ denotes the LBS content needed for an query q which is submitted by vehicle v at the time t.

From the above equations, it can be observed that the value of $\tau_t^{v,q}$ is determined by c_t^v which is actually decided by c_t^r. Therefore, the broadcasting content of the RSU is the decisive factor of the privacy preservation problem. On the other hand, as the queries are randomly generated, it is not possible to obtain the optimal value of c_t^r with a closed-form expression. Therefore, we will introduce our proposed scheme to solve the problem in the following two subsections, based on adaptive- and knowledge-based pre-caching methods, respectively.

5.3.4 Privacy-Enhancing Scheme Based on LBS Content Broadcasting and Active Caching (LBS-CBAC)

Algorithm 1 explains the proposed privacy preservation scheme in detail, which includes operations of both RSU and OBU on the vehicular.

(1) RSU Content Updating and Broadcasting:

At the very beginning time t_0, we assume there is no information about the content needed to be broadcasted for all RSUs. Therefore, $I_{t_0}^{r,p} = 0, \forall p \in \mathscr{P}, \forall r \in \mathscr{R}$. Also, we calculate the maximal number of POIs P_B^r, which could be broadcasted to a vehicle passing the RSU at the time t. (**Line 1 in Algorithm 3**)

Algorithm 3: LBS-CBAC

---

1 **Initialization:** $I_{t_0}^{r,p} = 0$, $P_B^r = \left\lfloor \frac{C_{t,max}^r}{C^p} \right\rfloor$, $\forall r \in \mathscr{R}$, $\forall p \in \mathscr{P}$, $\forall t \in \mathscr{T}$, $\forall q \in \mathscr{Q}$.

2 *RSU Content Updating and Broadcasting*:

3 **for** $r \in \mathscr{R}$ **do**

4   **if** *r received the query q* **then**

5   **if** $c^p \subseteq c_t^{v,q}$ **then**

6   **if** $\sum\limits_{p \in \mathscr{P}} I_t^{r,p} \leq P_B^r$ **then**

7                  $I_t^{r,p} = 1$.

8   **end**

9   **else**

10   Select a c^{p_0} which satisfies $I_t^{r,p_0} == 1$ by FIFO or LRU scheme;

11                  $I_t^{r,p_0} = 0$;

12                  $I_t^{r,p} = 1$.

13   **end**

14   **end**

15   **end**

16   Broadcast c_t^r with data rate η^r.

17 **end**

18 *OBU Active Caching*:

19 **for** $v \in \mathscr{V}$ **do**

20   **while** *v is within communication zone of r* **do**

21   Download c_t^r;

22          $c_t^v = c_t^v \bigcup c_t^r$.

23   **end**

24   **while** $c_t^{v,q} \neq \emptyset$ **do**

25   **if** $c_t^{v,q} \subseteq c_t^v$ **then**

26   Return all c^p related to q.

27   **end**

28   **else**

29   Send q to next accessible r.

30   **end**

31   **end**

32 **end**

When a vehicle v issues a query q, if the LBS content for the query is not contained in its own OBU, it forwards the query to the nearest RSU if accessible. For the RSU which receives the query, it updates the broadcasting buffer accordingly. Here, we should notice that each query q actually requires multiple POI information c^p; e.g., we may want the information of ten best restaurants near a certain location. (**Line 5–14 in Algorithm 3**)

Specifically, when updating the RSU broadcasting content, we have to make sure that the data volume does not exceed the maximal size P_B^r (**Line 6 in Algorithm 1**); otherwise, some old data should be replaced, using either the first in, first out (FIFO) or the least recent used (LRU) methods (**Line 10 in Algorithm 3**).

(2) OBU Active Caching:

A vehicular receives some POI information when it passes an RSU and merges these information into its own OBU cache (**Line 20–23 in Algorithm 3**).

At the same time, whenever there is a query q issued by the user in the vehicle, the OBU is checked and then either responds with POI information or forwards this query to the nearest RSU (**Line 24–30 in Algorithm 3**).

5.3.5   Knowledge-Based Pre-caching for RSU Broadcasting Content

In the above scheme, we update the RSU broadcasting content according to the received queries. If we could obtain the query probabilities in different locations by either mathematical model or training, then the RSUs' caches can be filled according to the priori knowledge.

Using the probability defined in Eq. (5.3), our knowledge-based pre-caching (KBPC) method is illustrated in Algorithm 4. Then when a user in vehicle v sends a query q, as v is in the communication zone and p is included in the query result for q, thus we have $Prob(l_p, l_r) \approx Prob(l_q, l_v)$. Therefore, the content in RSU broadcasting buffer will satisfy the queries with high probability.

Algorithm 4: KBPC for RSU Content Broadcasting

---
1 **for** $r \in \mathscr{R}$ **do**
2   **for** $p \in \mathscr{P}$ **do**
3 | Calculate $Prob(l_p, l_r)$;
4   **end**
5   Sort elements in $c_{t_0}^r$ in non-increasing order according to corresponding $Prob(l_p, l_r)$;
6   Set $I_{t_0}^{r,p} = 1$ for the first P_B^r elements in $c_{t_0}^r$; Broadcast $c_{t_0}^r$ with data rate η^r.
7 **end**

5.4   Performance Evaluation

5.4.1   Simulation Setup

The empirical evaluation is performed using the SimpleGeo Places dataset that contains information of more that 20 million places around the world, and is distributed under the creative commons open license [10]. The Australia part of the dataset has 697,653 entries, with data corresponding to multiple business categories and subcategories. Entries are maintained in the GeoJSON format and include attributes such

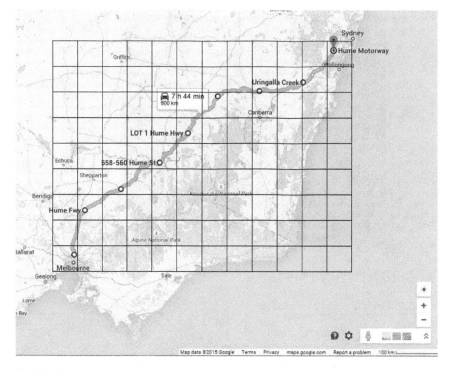

Fig. 5.4 Map of the area for simulation (white circles indicate the positions of RSUs when $d_{rsu} =$ 100 km)

as names, latitudes/longitudes, addresses, phone numbers, classifiers (category, type, subcategory), and tags.

We choose an 800 km-long section of the M31 highway connecting Melbourne and Sydney which is the busiest highway in Australia. The 600 km × 450 km area which covers this highway is divided into 9 × 12 50 km × 50 km small cells, as shown in Fig. 5.4. We use these cells to simplify the calculation of POI query probabilities which are related to the distance. There are totally 250,755 POI entries in this area, and the distribution in each cell is illustrated by Fig. 5.5. Our proposed LBS-CBAC scheme is simulated with different groups of parameters listed in Table 5.3.

We use both adaptive (FIFO, LRU)- and the knowledge-based pre-caching methods to update the RSU content, and 1,000,000 queries are generated for each simulation. For every vehicle v which issues the query q, its current position and the position it entered the highway are randomly generated. RSUs located between the current position and entering position are assumed to have broadcasted their contents to the OBU. And the queried locations are generated according to the current position and probabilities defined in Eq. (5.3). Figure 5.6 gives an example of query probabilities for different cells when the current location is the same with one of the nine RSUs.

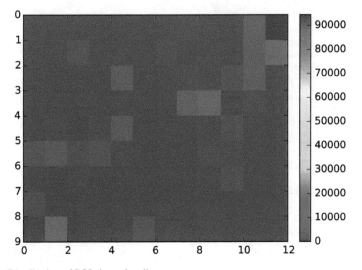

Fig. 5.5 Distribution of POIs in each cell

Table 5.3 Parameters used in simulations

Parameter	Value
Channel occupancy	1, 0.8, 0.5, 0.2
RSU distance d_{rsu} (km)	100*, 50
Vehicular velocity v (km/h)	110*, 60
POI entry size C^p (Kbits)	4.8†, 2.4, 1.2, 0.6, 0.3
POI query set size	10, 20†, 50, 100
Maximum app layer data rate η_{max} (Mbps)	2
RSU communication zone ζ (m)	1000

†Actual size of geojson format data is 4.8 Kbits which is used as default value if not specifically mentioned. * Default values of d_{rsu}, vehicular velocity, and POI query set size are, 100 km, 110 km/h, and 20, respectively, if not specifically mentioned.

5.4.2   Performance Analysis

Figures 5.7, 5.8, 5.9, 5.10, and 5.11 outline the impacts of different parameters on the privacy degree. Detailed analysis is provided in the following part.

(1) Channel Occupancy: Channel occupancy represents the communication cost in our proposed scheme. Figure 5.7 shows that the privacy degree of our scheme increases with the channel occupancy, no matter what method is used to update RSU content. However, the relationship between the privacy degree and the channel occupancy is not linear as the probabilities of queried POIs are not equal. Take the pre-cache method as an example, the privacy degree is about 0.4 when 20% of the DSRC SCH throughput is used and the figure only rises to roughly 0.6 when all the

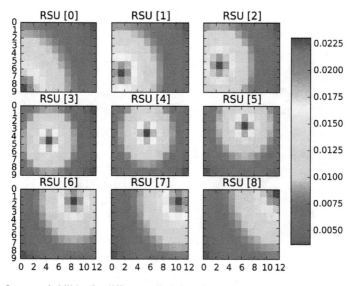

Fig. 5.6 Query probabilities for different cells (when the current location is the same as one of the nine RSUs when $d_{rsu} = 100\,\mathrm{km}$)

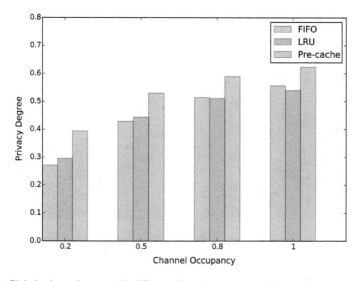

Fig. 5.7 Global privacy degrees with different channel occupancy values

SCH throughput is occupied. It indicates that only broadcasting the hot POIs is more efficient with regard to the communication cost.

(2) RSU Distance: Smaller RSU distance means more RSUs in the area and consequentially more content delivered by the RSUs, as shown in Fig. 5.8. But as all RSUs intend to active broadcast the popular POI information, the double of

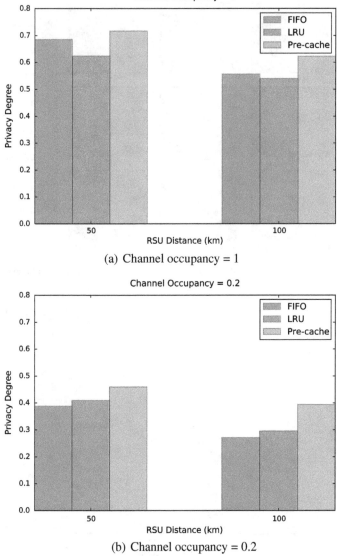

(a) Channel occupancy = 1

(b) Channel occupancy = 0.2

Fig. 5.8 Global privacy degrees with different RSU distances

RSU number does not actually double the achievable privacy degree. As shown in Fig. 5.8a, the privacy degrees of FIFO method are approximately 0.68 and 0.56 when RSU distances are 50 and 100 km, respectively.

(3) Vehicular Velocity: The effect of the vehicular speed is similar to that of the RSU distance. When a vehicle is moving slower, the sojourn time becomes longer; thus, the OBU could download more content from the RSU. For example, as shown

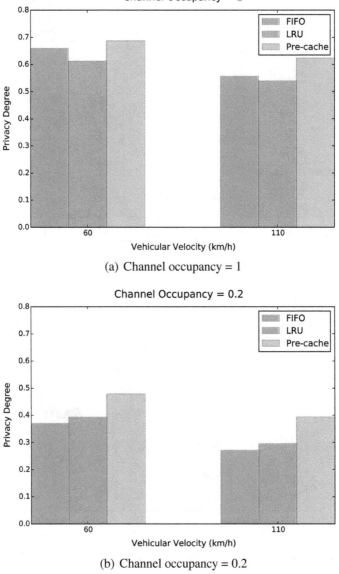

(a) Channel occupancy = 1

(b) Channel occupancy = 0.2

Fig. 5.9 Global privacy degrees with different vehicular velocities

in Fig. 5.9a, the privacy degrees of FIFO method are around 0.66 and 0.56 when vehicular velocities are 60 and 110 km/h, respectively.

(4) POI Entry Size: As shown in Fig. 5.10, reducing POI entry size has positive impact on the privacy degree. When the volume of entry drops from 4.8 Kbits to 2.4 Kbits, the privacy degree is improved from about 0.56 to 0.67, using FIFO method.

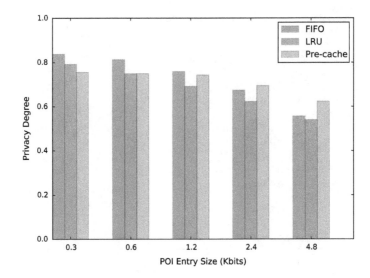

Fig. 5.10 Global privacy degrees with different POI entry sizes

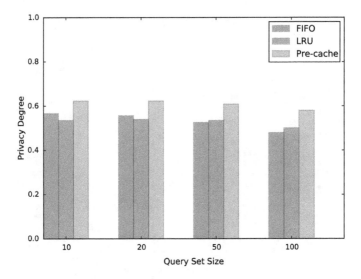

Fig. 5.11 Global privacy degrees with different query set sizes

It means that if we could introduce more efficient data format or data compression technique, the privacy degree of the proposed scheme could be improved.

(5) Query Set Size: Query set size is the number of POIs returned to an LBS query. It has a slight effect on the privacy degree. Only that too big set such as 100 introduces possible useless content broadcasting. As shown in Fig. 5.11, the best query set size is 20 when using default values for other parameters.

(6) RSU Content Update Method: The performances of three different RSU content update methods including FIFO, LRU, and knowledge-based pre-cache are compared in Figs. 5.7, 5.8, 5.9, 5.10, and 5.11. In most cases, knowledge-based pre-caching method has the best performance (in Figs. 5.7, 5.8, and 5.9), because this method tries to store the hottest POIs in RSU caches for broadcasting. However, this may cause some content overlap between different RSUs, which brings the performance bottleneck when the privacy degree is comparably high. As shown in Fig. 5.10, the performance of FIFO exceeds that of the pre-cache method when their privacy degrees approaching 0.8. It is because that FIFO will store all previous queried POIs in RSU caches which actually increases the diversity of POIs in different RSUs.

5.4.3 Comparison of Privacy Level with k-Anonymity Methods

In this subsection, we compare the effectiveness of the proposed method with the k-anonymity methods.

Although entropy has often been used to evaluate the performance of k-anonymous methods [11], it is not suitable to use an entropy metric here, as in our framework, the privacy of a user is either disclosed or completely protected.

Instead, we could use our defined privacy degree metric to evaluate the k-anonymity methods. A mobile user is considered location k-anonymous if and only if the location information sent to the service provider is made indistinguishable from that of at least $(k-1)$ other users. Therefore, the probability of the user being identified is $1/k$ whenever one query is issued. This is equivalent to the case that averagely one location privacy will be leaked among every k queries. Thus, the privacy degree is $\frac{k-1}{k}$.

Figure 5.12 outlines the privacy degree with different values of k, along with some typical privacy degree values using our proposed scheme. In our highway scenario, the general distance Ψ_{follow} between two consecutive cars is around 300 meters at busy time. Assuming they communicate via the V2V channel (communication distance is less than 500 meters) to form a group, it is very difficult to achieve a high k-anonymity. For example, M31 which is used in our simulation has two lanes in each direction in most part, one for normal driving and the other for overtaking. Thus, there are generally 2–3 cars which could communicate with each other to form an anonymity community. Then, the privacy degree is at most 66.7%, which is still lower than that achieved via the proposed scheme. Moreover, this figure will be further reduced when the road is not busy.

Finally, our proposed scheme is not conflict with the k-anonymity methods. Actually, these methods can be used at the same time to further enhance users' privacy.

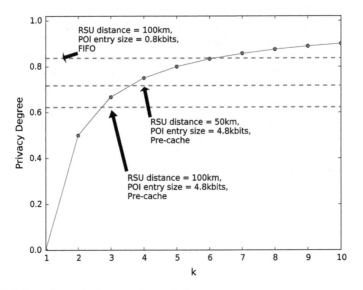

Fig. 5.12 Privacy degree for k-anonymity methods

5.4.4   Further Discussions

Besides anonymity methods, other existing privacy preservation methods can be used together with our proposed approach as well. To be more specific, our proposed scheme is based on the idea of "reducing the number of queries," while other methods such as cryptographic systems can help preserving privacy when there are "some queries we have to submit." As can be seen in the simulation part, it is generally not possible to eliminate all the queries. Therefore, the combination of these different approaches is an interesting future research topic.

With regard to the possibility of eliminating all the queries, we consider it as a tradeoff issue. It can be seen that in our simulation results, the highest privacy degree is around 80%. Theoretically, the privacy degree could approach 100% with higher data rate, denser RSUs, and smaller POI entry sizes. The extreme case is that the RSU pushes all the possible POI information to the OBU's cache. Thus, it is a balance between the cost and the privacy degree.

Another tradeoff in our scheme exists between the privacy degree and the RSU power consumption. Considering that the broadcasting is always more efficient when there are more users at the same time, we can improve our algorithm by setting a certain threshold; i. e., the broadcasting starts to work when there are more than n users in a certain area. This will help us to balance between the privacy preservation and the power consumption.

One more issue we would like to discuss is the situation of cellular-enabled vehicular network. Basically, we could use the same scheme, except that the RSU's function is performed by the cellular BS, and some parameters such as the data rate and the communication zone will change accordingly.

5.5 Conclusions

In this paper, we have studied the privacy issue of location-based service applications in wireless vehicular networks. Based on the DSRC standard, we have proposed the framework to enhance the privacy of LBS by active caching. Our contributions are threefold. First, we have developed the POI query probability model based on space-related feature of LBS queries from in-vehicle users. In addition, three RSU broadcasting content selection algorithms are proposed, including two adaptive updating methods and one knowledge-based pre-caching method. Based on the above framework, we have analyzed the impacts of important parameters on the privacy degree, including RSU distance, vehicle speed, POI query set size, size of each POI entry, and the proportion of channel capacity used for RSU broadcast (defined as channel occupancy). Detailed simulation results and performance analysis have validated that the proposed scheme can protect the privacy by reducing the number of queries needed for LBSs. Moreover, our proposed method can be combined with the existing cryptography-based or anonymity-based methods to further enhance the privacy in the vehicular networks.

References

1. B. Liu, W. Zhou, T. Zhu, L. Gao, T.H. Luan, H. Zhou, Silence is golden: enhancing privacy of location-based services by content broadcasting and active caching in wireless vehicular networks. IEEE Trans. Veh. Technol. **65**(12), 9942–9953 (2016)
2. B. Niu, Q. Li, X. Zhu, G. Cao, H. Li, Enhancing privacy through caching in location-based services, in *Proceedings of the IEEE INFOCOM* (2015)
3. J.B. Kenney, Dedicated short-range communications (DSRC) standards in the united states. Proc. IEEE **99**(7), 1162–1182 (2011)
4. *IEEE Std 802.11p-2010, IEEE Standard for Information Technology– Local and Metropolitan Area Networks– Specific Requirements– Part 11: Wireless LAN Medium Access Control (MAC) and Physical Layer (PHY) Specifications Amendment 6: Wireless Access in Vehicular Environments* (2010), pp. 1–51
5. M.I. Hassan, H.L. Vu, T. Sakurai, Performance analysis of the ieee 802.11 MAC protocol for DSRC safety applications. IEEE Trans. Veh. Technol. **60**(8), 3882–3896 (2011)
6. *IEEE P1609.3-2010, IEEE Standard for Wireless Access in Vehicular Environments (WAVE)* (2010), pp. 1–11
7. X. Yin, X. Ma, K.S. Trivedi, A. Vinel, Performance and reliability evaluation of bsm broadcasting in DSRC with multi-channel schemes. IEEE Trans. Comput. **63**(12), 3101–3113 (2014)
8. R. Shokri, G. Theodorakopoulos, J.-Y. Le Boudec, J.-P. Hubaux, Quantifying location privacy. Proc. IEEE Secur. Priv. 247–262 (2011)
9. R. Shokri, J. Freudiger, M. Jadliwala, J.-P. Hubaux, A distortion-based metric for location privacy, in *Proceedings of the ACM Workshop on Privacy in the Electronic Society* (2009), pp. 21–30
10. SimpleGeo Pulic Spaces CC0 Colletion (2011), https://archive.org/details/2011-08-SimpleGeo-CC0-Public-Spaces
11. A. Serjantov, G. Danezis, *Towards an Information Theoretic Metric for Anonymity* (2003), pp. 41–53

Chapter 6
Future Directions and Conclusions

In this chapter, we will discuss the future directions in location privacy research and summarize this book.

6.1 Future Directions

6.1.1 Location Privacy Protection Under Correlations

Although the location privacy issues have been widely studied, most previous studies have focused on independent data, which assume that all data were independently sampled from a universe. Despite this, a real-world dataset often exhibits strong coupling relations, where some records are frequently correlated with each other, and this may disclose more information than expected. Some research is beginning to account for the temporal and spatial correlations in location data [1–3], but these efforts are far from mature.

A further challenge is the correlation between location data and other databases. For example, health and medical records may be associated with people's location information to launch attacks. This is an important direction of research but has not yet been well-studied.

6.1.2 Location Privacy in Big Data and Deep Learning Era

The massive amounts of data available on the Internet and the unprecedented accuracy of deep learning methods are continually reshaping many areas of research and industry. At the same time, these methods present obvious privacy issues [4]. For example, current deep learning-based methods can detect type of objects [5] and

© The Author(s), under exclusive licence to Springer Nature Singapore Pte Ltd. 2018   99
B. Liu et al., *Location Privacy in Mobile Applications*,
SpringerBriefs on Cyber Security Systems and Networks,
https://doi.org/10.1007/978-981-13-1705-7_6

recognize celebrities and landmarks from personal photos posted on social networks. These methods can automatically collect and process millions of photos or videos to reveal private information. For example, Weyand et al. [6] were able to predict the geo-locations of users with high accuracy just from their personal photos.

Traditional privacy preservation methods seem powerless when faced with large-scale deep learning tools and a Big Data training set. Hence, location privacy problems need to be reinvestigated in a Big Data and deep learning context.

6.1.3 Location Privacy in Autonomous Systems

Another important research direction is location privacy in some complicated system, such as the autonomous systems (driverless car). Driverless vehicles are fast emerging and will become mainstream transportation in the near future. It is predicted that 10 million self-driving cars will hit the road by 2020. These driverless vehicles bring various benefits to individuals and the society at large by greatly increasing the efficiency, safety, and functionality of transport systems.

Existing privacy protection methods cannot handle the privacy protection problem in driverless vehicle systems due to complex data features, nor can they be easily extended or modified to tackle this problem. For instance, the accurate real-time data cannot be handled by privacy protection methods based on anonymization and obfuscation as they will result in considerable information loss. Encryption-based methods are not applicable either due to their high computational complexity and latency. These methods cannot deal with correlated and unstructured data either as they require the data to be independent and structured. Therefore, we need to develop novel privacy protection techniques for driverless vehicle systems.

6.2 Conclusions

The privacy issue raises people's attention again, with the Facebook privacy scandal occupying the recent headlines of major media. Among the different types of data, location data coming along with the growth of location-based services (LBSs) in mobile applications raise severe privacy concerns as it is used frequently in everyone's daily life.

Despite the big amount of papers in this area, there lacks a systematic study to present all related components of the problem. Moreover, the gap between theory and practice is big. To overcome these obstacles, we provide an integrated five-element framework for location privacy research in this book, which includes analysis of location privacy definitions, attacks and adversaries, location privacy protection methods, location privacy metrics, and location-based mobile applications. In addition, location privacy issue has been studied in detail in three different applications, showing how this privacy problem can be tackled with in real life. We also share some insights on the possible research directions. We believe that the location privacy research will see a great boom in the coming years.

References

1. A.-M. Olteanu, K. Huguenin, R. Shokri, M. Humbert, J.-P. Hubaux, Quantifying interdependent privacy risks with location data. IEEE Trans. Mob. Comput. **16**(3), 829–842 (2017)
2. L. Ou, Z. Qin, Y. Liu, H. Yin, Y. Hu, H. Chen, Multi-user location correlation protection with differential privacy, in *Proceedings of the IEEE 22nd International Conference on Parallel and Distributed Systems (ICPADS)* (2016), pp. 422–429
3. L. Fan, L. Xiong, An adaptive approach to real-time aggregate monitoring with differential privacy. IEEE Trans. Knowl. Data Eng. **26**(9), 2094–2106 (2014)
4. A. Mehmood, I. Natgunanathan, Y. Xiang, G. Hua, S. Guo, Protection of big data privacy. IEEE Access **4**, 1821–1834 (2016)
5. S. Ren, K. He, R. Girshick, J. Sun, Faster R-CNN: towards real-time object detection with region proposal networks. IEEE Trans. Pattern Anal. Mach. Intell. **39**(6), 1137–1149 (2017)
6. T. Weyand, I. Kostrikov, J. Philbin, Planet-photo geolocation with convolutional neural networks, in *European Conference on Computer Vision* (Springer, Berlin, 2016), pp. 37–55